THE ATTACHMENT CYCLE

An Object Relations Approach
to the Healing Ministries

Michael J. Garanzini, S.J.

■ Paulist Press ■
New York / Mahwah

To my parents, my first teachers;
and to Professor Edward V. Stein, my most recent

■

Book design by Ellen Whitney

Copyright 1988 by Michael J. Garanzini, S.J.

Library of Congress Cataloging-in-Publication Data

Garanzini, Michael J., 1948–
   The attachment cycle : an object relations approach to healing ministries / by Michael J. Garanzini.
      p. cm.
   Bibliography: p.
   Includes index.
   ISBN 0-8091-2970-1 (pbk.)
   1. Attachment behavior. 2. Object relations (Psychoanalysis)
3. Identity (Psychology) 4. Pastoral psychology. 5. Spiritual
healing. I. Title.
BF575 A86G27   1988
616.89'1—dc 19   88-2479
                                                  CIP

Published by Paulist Press
997 Macarthur Boulevard
Mahwah, NJ 07430

Printed and bound in the
United States of America

■ TABLE OF CONTENTS ■

Introduction ■ 1

1 ■ **Ministry and Discipleship:**
Toward a Theology of Healing 13

2 ■ **The ASL-R Cycle in Psychodynamic
Theory:** The Role of Instincts 33

3 ■ **Human Relationship in the Developmental
Process:** The Contributions of Sullivan
and Klein 56

4 ■ **The Developmental Cycle in Object
Relations Theory:** The Contributions of
Mahler, Winnicott and Fairbairn 78

5 ■ **The Development of Self-Esteem:** Object
Relations Theory and the Role of Therapy 99

6 ■ **The Attachment Cycle and Therapy:** Three Case
Illustrations 115

7 ■ **Overall Summary and Conclusions** 159

Notes 167

Bibliography 179

Indexes 185

▪ TABLES AND DRAWINGS ▪

Margaret Mahler's Timeline: Table 1   82

The Attachment-Separation-Loss and Re-birth
Cycle in Therapy: Table 2   130

Case One: Drawings of Henry   120

Case Two: Drawings of William   135

Case Three: Drawings of Agnes   147

■ INTRODUCTION ■

Whose Am I? ■ ■

■ While on a bus I overheard a conversation between a man and his son which impressed upon me the importance of the attachment bond. Apparently, this young boy, about four years of age, had been asking his father about family relationships. "Are you Karen's daddy, then?" the boy asked. "No, I'm not," responded the father. "Then you should be," retorted the son. Tickled by this, the boy's father said, "She belongs to Uncle Leo." "And I'm yours?" asked the child, seeking reassurance that he was comprehending all this. "Yes, you're mine." Ana-Marie Rizzuto tells of a similar story concerning an adult. After being away from her hometown in Eastern Europe, a fifty-six year old woman was asked while shopping in the town marketplace, "Whose are you?"[1]

The issue of belonging is something that stays with us throughout our lifetime. Being a part of a network, of a group, of something bigger than our solitary existence is crucial for survival—physical, psychic and spiritual. Our identity, the way we perceive ourselves and the way others perceive us, is inextricably linked to our attachments to others.

The question of belonging hits at the fundamental issue of human relatedness and concerns ultimately the questions which have often been identified as "religious," that is, questions of the meaning and value of our life with one another. The minister and the therapist have a special interest in this question and in the process whereby it is understood and facilitated. And, perhaps more important, they share a special concern when the process of relationship has been torn, stalled or injured in some way. Thus, minister and therapist are concerned with the healing process on both the intrapsychic and interpsychic levels.

This thesis seeks to explore the contributions of several the-

1

orists in the object relations school of psychodynamic thought who have attempted to elucidate the fundamental nature of human relatedness. These theorists have focused their attention on the attachment bond between children and their parents. By implication, they offer a way of discussing and understanding the relationship process throughout the life cycle. Since ministry is a "caring for persons," the contribution of object relations theorists to our understanding of the relational process holds the potential for elucidating a theology of healing, especially when the healing of relationships is at the heart of this ministry.

In addition, the experience of Christians who have over the centuries taken ministry-to-persons seriously may help contribute to a clearer understanding of the therapeutic process as it seeks to restore people to their optimum in love, work and relating to one another in community. This type of exploration is not new. Pastoral psychologists and theologians have long searched for commonalities and possible contributions coming from psychodynamic theory and therapy. This cross-pollination process has been fruitful, especially for pastoral ministry. The more recent phenomenon in psychodynamic theory of a sustained focus on the object relations of individuals and its lifetime effects offers new information contributing toward our understanding of ministry. It sheds new light on the nature of growth and development, as well as the healing that takes place in the pastoral relationship.

A theology of ministry and healing and psychodynamic theory are partners in this endeavor. There is a third aspect as well which will be important for consideration. This source involves the case materials from therapy with children and families who have come to seek help in understanding the difficuties experienced in important relationships which are not "functioning" as hoped or expected. These case studies are an important source of data for elucidating the theories of ministry and psychodynamic relationship processes, and for examining the relevance of some of the concepts which come from these two fields of study.

These cases are also proof of the difficulty of change, of growth, and the pain that is necessary in much of the human development process. They are real-life examples of the cyclic process of separation from important attachments and the inevitable losses which each human being faces on the road to maturity.

They are examples of crises of development, of loss and the gain which arises out of loss. On the level of faith, as concrete examples of the movement of sin and grace in the lives of people, they are a manifestation of God's use of all things, evil included, for the good of his creatures.

The Method ▪▪

In their book, *Method in Ministry*, Evelyn and James Whitehead advocate a three-way conversation or dialogue for theological reflection. "Faithful and effective pastoral activity depends on the ability of Christians—and in a special way, Christian ministers—to recognize and use religiously significant insights available in ... three sources." These three sources are identified as including the Scriptures, cultural information, especially from the behavioral sciences, and personal experience. By attending, asserting and making decisions, information from these three sources is clarified and refined, coordinated and shaped into pastoral action.[2]

Theological reflection, then, involves a serious examination of the Church's experience and its reflection on the source of insights and truth, the Scriptures. In the case of pastoral action and ministry—of which therapy as a healing endeavor is one—how the Church understands the ministry of healing in traditional and scriptural terms will be one important element. While a detailed analysis of the pluriformity of the tradition and the history of the concept of healing in ministry cannot be given here, it will be enough to indicate, in general ways, what the tradition and the Scriptures tell us about the ministry of healing. Ministry as a topic of theological reflection is relatively new within some traditions, such as the Roman Catholic tradition, but the insights of pastoral theologians concerning the pastoral dimension of the Church's ministry is crucial, nevertheless.

This reflection also involves a serious consideration of the contributions of the wider culture. Healing in the therapeutic process has been the aim and concern of psychotherapists for some time. Theologians have reflected on its implication for pastoral ministry, and much has been written about the contributions of theorists such as Freud and Jung to the theology of pastoral ministry. Relatively little has been written about the contributions of one of the most significant branches, and one which is potentially a source of much information, the object relations school of thought. The contributions of this school or branch of psychodynamic theory to family therapy, to social psychology, and to pediatric medicine are emerging on a regular basis. The hope here is to explore the possible fruitfulness of considering object relations as a source for reflection on the ministry of healing relationships and inner hurts and wounds, traditionally seen as a therapeutic process, but as a pastoral one as well.

Finally, case materials which demonstrate the usefulness of this conversation toward a more informed theology of ministry and healing may shed some light on the dynamics involved in all ministry. If the object of ministry is the building up of the community of believers and the facilitating of the human and divine interaction in relationship, then the healing of relational ties, on a human level, ought to tell us something of the divine relationship to which all men and women are called.

Since the term "object relations" will be used throughout this study, it is important to clarify its significance and its meaning as a technical term in psychodynamic theory. In a real sense it is an unfortunate term since it seems, at first, to imply something which the religious tradition has long condemned—the focus of human interest and love on material goods. However, in psychodynamic theory it refers to a psychological process that all people use, early in life and throughout it, to create internalized images of the self and other people. These intended patterns and images are known as "object relations." The dynamic relationship between these inner structures creates the foundation for intimate relationships throughout one's life. The development of identity, the deepening of the capacity to endure frustration and fluctuation in intimate relationships, the growth of the ability to love and empathize, to be faithful and trusting, all stem—in the object relations view—from the quality and the durability of the people upon whom one depends. Understanding the way the child internalizes these experiences in the first years of life is crucial for understanding the way the individual or the way human beings in general conceive of themselves as individuals.[3]

With this clarification in place, it will be helpful to examine the general structure of this thesis before describing the conceptual model upon which it is based. The "road map" which follows takes us from Freud to Mahler and Kohut down one course and then through the ruminations of modern theologians. These underground and "aerial" explorations are brought onto *terra firma* when we examine some case materials within the therapeutic process in the final chapters.

Plan of Development ▪▪

Chapter One explores the nature and purpose of ministry and healing in psychotherapy. To the extent that ministry is a donation of self and a risk, it involves faith and trust. This faith exists on both the therapist's and the client's part. It is delicate and fragile and built up by the gradual unfolding of the client's story. Ministry involves, then, a sharing of one's life story which in fact is an entering into the life story of one in need. In this self-donation, pain and confusion are inevitable and, if the Gospel story is taken seriously, necessary. In attachment, separation and loss both the client and therapist discover that their stories are part of the quintessential story of salvation, the Jesus story.

Chapter Two attempts a serious examination of the issues of attachment, separation and loss as they have been conceived in traditional psychoanalytic literature. As psychodynamic process, they have been more or less specifically addressed since Freud. But a serious look at Freud's understanding of human nature as expressed in the theory of instincts, motivation and anxiety leads to the conclusion that conceiving of human drives as bent on satisfaction and discharge is flawed. Rather, there is considerable data to suggest that, from the beginning, human beings like much primate life in general are instinctively driven toward those to whom we are given. That is, we are fundamentally social and not secondarily so as Freud and his chief followers would have us believe.

From this point of view, a more comprehensive theory of "human life in relationship" can be constructed. Chapter Three explores the work of H. S. Sullivan and Melanie Klein, two pioneers of psychoanalytically oriented psychotherapy. Both drew on Freud but modified his theory in significant ways. Sullivan stressed the interpsychic and Klein the intrapsychic. While their ideas and contributions are slanted in particular directions, taken together they contribute to a theoretical position that takes both the relational and the internal dynamics of attachment to others seriously.

A more complete and comprehensive appreciation of the unfolding of the attachment drive is the chief concern of those theorists and researchers known as object relations theorists, Mahler, Winnicott and Fairbairn in particular. Our exploration of their work in Chapter Four has the purpose of examining the maturation process in children and yields at least two other results: (a) a way of appreciating the cyclical process of attachment, separation and loss as a requisite for "rebirth"; (b) a model for conceiving how this rebirth process functions in therapy. If the therapeutic alliance serves the purpose of healing wounds, then it must approach the requirements of genuine care and trust which original parental bonds were meant to foster.

Chapter Five takes us more deeply into the issue and the mystery called "the self." The focus here is on self-concept and self-esteem development. This approach is helpful for a more complete explanation and appreciation of what constitutes psychopathology, seen here as a wounded self. If attachment figures or the environment in general has been unable to foster healthy development of relationships, then negotiating attachments, separations and losses is usually impossible as serious blows to self-concept and poor self-esteem regulation are likely to occur. At heart then is a damaged capacity for intimacy or mutuality, manifesting itself in neurotic and even psychotic behavior. The child's wounded self is in need of healing through care—the goal of therapy.

The Growth Cycle ▪▪

The plan then is to offer a model of human development and maturation that sees human relationship as a natural and intrinsic urge in the human being. Sullivan, Klein, Mahler and other object relations theorists offer the most useful framework for conceiving of the psychological growth of the human person in attachment terms. Specifically, the model to which these theorists contribute proposes that attachments lead inevitably to separation which brings anxiety, a fuel, if you will, for the growth process. Separations lead inevitably to loss, at least loss of the object or person in the old way of relating. Through separation and loss the human being is challenged to accept the other as truly "other" and not simply as object-for-me. This is crucial for discovering, accepting and even rejoicing in the world which is not-me, which is other. Sullivan, Klein and Mahler, plus the contributions of Winnicott and Fairbairn, have stressed individuation and maturation in ways which illuminate this growth of a self-in-relationship.

The pain of separation and loss is crucial for the unfolding of the developmental process. Because of separation and loss, a reappraisal of the "object" is not only possible but necessary. When allowed to negotiate the pain of separation and loss, the human being becomes more aware of who and what he or she is as a person. The development of a sense of self—as distinct from ego accomplishments—is dependent on these separation and loss cycles. The growth of a realistic, and healthy sense of self is dependent, moreover, on healthy attachments and processes such as mirroring and internalizing the attachment figure. This movement from attachment, leading to separation and finally to loss, can be traced in the psychological as well as in the spiritual realm.

This exploration begins with an examination of a pastoral theology of ministry, especially the ministry of healing. The writing of Congar, Rahner and Schillebeeckx, in the Roman tradition, have crystalized the Church's understanding of effective and important ministry. But additional important considerations arise out of the ministry of Jesus in the cure of persons seen in the Gospel accounts. From this reflection a clue to the nature of healing emerges. Healing involves an outside source, an "other" who extends care and compassion. It involves as well an unexplained and unforced response whereby the wounded "accepts" at some core level the offer of a cure. At heart, healing is always a healing of the wounded self.

Once this theological reflection is in place, we will then be in a position to examine the way key concepts in our model of development and growth have been handled in the literature. That is, we will examine the attachment, separation and loss dynamic in psychoanalytic theory. Beginning with Freud, psychodynamic theory has been concerned about the role of motivation, instincts and the role they play in intrapsychic life, and the problems of anxiety which develop due to separation and loss of important people.

Since it is a self that is developed in the cycle of attachments, separations and losses, and a self that emerges more whole and intact in the struggle from loss to new life, the importance of the growth, development and maintenance of a healthy self-concept, or self-esteem, will be the final topic raised in this first section. A cohesive self is understood and experienced as the author and main character of a life story. This narrative character of the self is illuminated by both a theology of story and a theory of therapy.

In Chapter Six the process and the problems of therapy with children and their families will be examined. Through the presentation of case materials concerning the therapy of several children, four to fourteen in age, this examination will show how the Attached, Separation, Loss and Rebirth (ASL-R) model sheds light on a host of problems such as the dynamic existing between therapist and child as the attachment, separation, and loss cycle is initiated and negotiated in the transference and countertransference. Again, all of this occurs against the backdrop of a theology of ministry and healing which sets the stage for conceiving of the therapeutic process in light of the Attachment, Separation, Loss and Re-Attachment Cycle (ASL-R Cycle) making it fundamentally a pastoral model as well as a psychotherapeutic one.

The use of art in therapy is not a new topic and has been extensively treated (see Chapter Six, "Introductory Remarks"). The symbolic nature of artistic productions and the "evidence" which such productions yield for the therapist will also be discussed.

A fascinating and encouraging aspect of the model proposed here is that the artistic productions of children during the course of therapy give "evidence" of the internal dynamics and struggle for health and wholeness. Often this struggle mirrors the ASL-R Cycle. These illustrations of the intrapsychic healing processes will be presented throughout this later section.

Most important is the way the therapeutic process enables the client to tell his or her story, to discover its meaning or meanings, and to better grasp the significance of being both its author and its main character. Object relations theory and a theology of ministry, healing and narration are partners here in helping our understanding and appreciation of the healing process in therapy. To complete this introduction however, it may be useful to say more about the way "attachment" is understood in psychodynamic theory.

The Conceptual Model and the Bonding Process ▪▪

Attachment, as a psychological and physiological concept, can be described as any form of behavior that results in a person's attaining or maintaining proximity to some other clearly identifiable individual conceived as better able to cope with the world. The most obvious example of attachment behavior is the frightened child assuaged by the comforting and care of a maternal figure. Crucial for the psychological health of such a child is the "knowledge" that the attachment figure is available and will be responsive. Insecurity and neurotic defenses against the threat of reality develop in children when care-giving figures are chronically absent or are present but cannot provide the sense of security which allows the child to value the relationship, to trust it, to continue to invest in it emotionally.

Attachment behavior is easily identifiable in children, but present throughout the life cycle. As Klaus and Kennell in their work, *Maternal Infant Bonding*, have stated, "The original mother-infant bond is the well-spring for all the infant's subsequent attachments and is the formative relationship in the course of which the child develops a sense of himself. Throughout his lifetime the strength and character of this attachment will influence the future bonds to other individuals."[4] These authors stress the long-lasting effect of this early attachment and the notion of sensitive and critical periods, beginning with the first few months when the mother-infant bond develops.

But the story is incomplete if one concentrates on the attachment process to the exclusion of other dynamics involved in human relationships. Early attachments are crucial to the formation of a rudimentary sense of self, as Ainsworth, Stroufe and others have stressed. Other elements are, for example, a necessary reciprocity within relationships which gives the child a first sense of what emotional availability and sensitivity to others entails. Most important, there are inevitable separations and losses which are crucial for growth and maturation.[5]

Because of this stress on the quality of the relationship between mother and infant and its effect on later growth and mental health, psychologists and psychoanalysts, in particular, have reexamined the Freudian assumptions surrounding the nature of human intrapsychic life as well as interpsychic reality. Freud gave the impetus to the work of Harlow, Mahler, Spitz, Bowlby, Ainsworth, Stroufe and many others who have more carefully studied the interpsychic life of infants and their maternal care-givers. Today, the infant is viewed as more than biologically "tied" to its mother for the purposes of care. These newer psychological theorists have expanded our notion of human sociability. As Helen B. Lewis has written recently, "A modern theoretical system based on the primacy of human social life, that is to say, human emotional bonds, has emerged within psychoanalysis challenging the older Freudian paradigm."[6]

In *Totem and Taboo*, Freud struggled with the question of how humans universally create a society ruled by moral law, evidence of his concern for the dynamics inherent in the human biological and psychological makeup that sociability is a "given." Lewis gives several reasons for the slow progress in constructing a scientific theory of innate human emotional connectedness.

First, Freud conceptualized that human emotions, as well as the ideas that represent them, are instinctual. "In using ideas as a unit of theorizing," Lewis feels, "Freud was following Locke's format that the mind is a box containing ideas—the mental equivalents of Newtonian particles." This emphasis has led to a "scientific-mathematical" approach to the study of the human.[7] Also, Darwinian evolutionary theory led Freud and others to "adumbrate" what anthropologists now take for granted: moral laws, laws of human interaction are immanent in human society and thus in human nature.

Freud was the first to draw attention to the fact that emotional distress and mental illness are bound up with unconscious process and that these have roots in the early life of the child. Still, Lewis and others in growing numbers are shifting conceptual frameworks. For example, she has proposed that shame and guilt be seen as attachment emotions and has demonstrated the effectiveness of this approach for solving therapeutic difficulties in cases of depression.[8]

But Freud has not only offered a paradigm. He has, as well, delineated the issues and then pointed to the wide range of phenomena that a psychodynamic theory must address. Any sound theory of intrapsychic or interpsychic life must explain the nature and purpose of instinct, motivation, anxiety and the nature and scope of the developmental process. All of this impacts a theory of therapy and cure.

To focus our discussion, then, when dealing with troubled children and family system, the question arises: How ought we to conceive of the issues and the problem which we confront in therapy? The broader question—and the more important one for the purposes of therapy—is: How ought we to understand the child's inner life and the dilemmas he or she is facing? We are raising questions, then, about the fundamental dynamics of human growth and relatedness. This necessitates that we have a comprehensive theory of the nature and scope of human maturation and development. From his dealing with adult patients, Freud backed into an examination of infantile issues. His theory of early infantile development and the nature of the motivational processes has been examined and refined or rejected by psychodynamic psychologists since. Two schools of thought grew out of Freudian psychodynamic theory—the American interpersonal school of psychiatry represented especially by Harry Stack Sullivan, and the British school of object relations. Together, they provide us with an especially helpful approach to an elucidation of the problems faced by the young, and the not-so-young, engulfed in relationships from the very start. But before going into a deeper examination of psychodynamic thought, a close look at a theology of ministry and healing will give us an overview of the important dimensions involved in the cure and care of souls.

The Judaeo-Christian tradition has long stressed the fundamental problem in life as that of connectedness vs. estrangement in relationship—relationships between and among humans and those of the human with the Divine. It might be said that the business of theology is the business of elucidating the relationship of God with the creation and creatures among themselves. From a different point of view, theology seeks to illuminate the nature of God through a reflection of the presence of the Divine in human relationship. We move now to a reflection on the meaning of ministry (discipleship), healing, and narration, that is, the unfolding of one's life story within the Gospel story. As Navone has stated so succinctly: "Our life is the search for our own true story with a larger, universal story."[9]

▪ 1 ▪

MINISTRY AND DISCIPLESHIP:
Toward a Theology of Healing

Introduction ▪▪

▪ This chapter is a tentative exploration of three dimensions of a theology of healing relevant to the therapeutic process. First, it will examine some of the current theological writings concerning ministry. It is especially a theology of the ministry of reconciliation that helps establish how the therapist ministers to persons by participating in their struggle to comprehend, appreciate, and, when necessary, rectify the important attachment bonds in their lives. Next, a theology of healing puts into focus the essentials of the healing process where care becomes cure. Finally, notes taken from what has been called "narrative" theology help draw attention to the way life history, the given circumstances of individual lives and the interpretations of such circumstances and history, hopes and wishes, are visible in the individual's cycles of attachment, separation, loss and rebirth. This is true for both minister or therapist and for client.

The therapist who sees himself or herself as ministering to others is not only facilitating the interpretation of the client's life story, but also becomes a part of that story and so heals and is healed in the therapeutic process. This is particularly a "Christian ministry" when done in imitation of the Jesus story. And to the extent that this is made conscious, the ministry is explicitly a religious one.

Notes on the Theology of Ministry ▪▪

In *A Theology of Ministry*, Thomas O'Meara writes: "The Church is a collective ministry and it serves the multiform presence of grace in the diverse social consciousness of the world."[1] Ministry is carried on in the concrete historical situation wherever believers endeavor to carry out the Gospel injunction to love as Jesus loved. Ministry then is fundamentally the response of the Christian or the community of Christians to further the reign of God in time and space.

The kingdom, then, is the source, milieu and goal of all ministry (Congar). A theology of ministry is, at heart, a meditation on the nature and purpose of that kingdom. It is a reflection on the Spirit's activity in and through believers. It may be said to be a contemplative analysis of the working of grace in the world. Ministry then is accomplished by believers in a variety of situations and walks of life—depending on the character of and response to the Spirit's call. The model of such activity and response is always Jesus himself, whom John's Gospel describes as the servant-minister, and Mark's describes as the New Adam, the new kind of human being.

The goal of ministry, Congar, Schillebeeckx and Rahner have emphasized in recent times, is not the building up of the Church. Rather, its goal is the kingdom which cannot be equated with the Church, just as Israel's religious and national interests could not be equated in the Old Testament. The aim of ministry is the building and maintenance of the relationship of the individual with God and with others. It concerns then the process of salvation in individual lives, that is, the "becoming that which God's creative love intends" in the life of each person.[2] Those who see their lives as involved in such work may understand this to be the way they express their discipleship.

Following from this, ministry cannot be equated with official ministry, that is, with "office" in the community of believers. It is something more fundamental than the "work of the Church" in that it embraces all people whether in or outside the community of believers. Moreover, it is especially concerned with the healing of broken relationships and a restoration of bonds which may or may not be "within" the believing community.

14

Whenever ministry to others is operative in word, sign or activity, then we understand it in terms of the activity of grace. When words are shared, signs are given or celebrated, whenever human communication is such that it is facilitative of the good of the other, enchancing the potential for connectedness, then ministry may be said to characterize this work. Both psychotherapy and ministry seek the genuine growth and development "of the other." In theological language and from the perspective of faith, this reality involves the coincidence of the transcendental nature of Divinity, the eschatological nature of the kingdom and the incarnational reality of Jesus—coming together in the moment of assistance.[3]

Ministry then is a call to freedom, to something beyond and yet fundamental to the health of the person. This essential freedom is found in Jesus who was free to bind himself to the will of the Father and thus accept the inevitability of suffering and death in the service of the truth and love to which he came to witness. This is the "gift" of ministry to those who inhabit a broken world. In this is a revelation of the nature of the kingdom which Jesus announced. It is a freedom from fear, fear of not living, fear of the judgment of the law, fear of loneliness and rejection should the respect and admiration of others be lost. This freedom is not a license to do whatever one will, but a call to more authentic bonding with God and with others. The only thing to fear, then, is the one who can sever attachment to the Father, Jesus instructed his disciples. The source of Jesus' courage and strength—especially in times of difficulty and trial—was always his relationship to the Father. This union, the subject of Jesus' teaching in the last discourse in John and vividly portrayed in the passion accounts of Jesus as he met his sufferings and death alone, provides believers and ministers with an account, a model and example of that to which they are called and that which awaits all men and women in their most trying moments.[4]

While anxiety and fear mark the passion and death of Jesus, they are also confronted at the initiation of his mission and ministry. The temptations of Jesus in the desert are a confrontation with the fear of rejection, the retreat into self-aggrandizement, of loss of control or power. Ultimately, they signify the struggle of Jesus to settle the important questions: To what do I give myself?

To whom do I attach myself? What is my ultimate source of courage and that from which I draw the love I am asked to give?

In this way, the Scriptures provide the minister with the essential paradigm around which an identity is built. These paradigms have the function of "informing, influencing, and inspiring" ministers as they approach pastoral issues. J. M. Gustafson, in his article, "The Relation of the Gospel to the Moral Life," explains that "paradigms are basic models of a vision of life and inform the practice of life, from which flow certain consistent attitudes, outlooks (or onlooks), rules or norms of behavior and specific actions."[5] The outstanding models of ministry in the New Testament are, of course, Jesus himself and Paul.

Because the Scriptures are available to the community of believers in different times and different places, they continually serve the minister as a new source of inspiration and paradigmatic example. In the light of new experience and new environmental situations, the Scriptures take on new life.[6] The specific implications of the call to be a servant or minister, as, for example, one who releases others from fear, is heard in the concrete circumstances of the charism and the need of others who are given to us. The therapist or healer discovers the nature and purpose of healing in the life and death of Jesus, in his words and in the accounts of his healing of others, and "hears" these accounts in light of those given to his or her care, those seeking a cure. The therapist who, united with the believing, worshiping community, understands the healing work of therapy to be a life-giving imitation of the healing works of Jesus is then a minister even if not an officially ordained one.

The Criterion for Authentic Ministry ▪▪

The German theologian, Karl Rahner, sees ministry as characterized by four essential elements, if it is to be authentic. Rahner drew his "criterion" for ministry from an analysis of ministry as it functioned within the first Christian communities. For Rahner, authentic Christian ministry is not equated with sacral office; thus it is not only open to, but is the responsibility of all believers. Ministry is always in the service of the kingdom, whichever way that is perceived in particular circumstances and times. It is concerned with doing something with and for people, and so it involves communication (and with that, no doubt, comes misunderstanding) and concrete activity on behalf of others. Finally, ministry is universal and diverse. In other words, there are no automatically excluded activities or ways of operating as long as these meet the criteria of building up the kingdom or the reign of God.[7]

Edward Schillebeeckx echoes many of the same points when he writes that "what arises spontaneously in the community of Jesus is at the same time experienced as a gift of the Holy Spirit."[8] He notes the effort of Paul to add co-workers (teachers, prophets, and healers) to the rank of ministers in the community (1 Cor 3:9). There, Paul initiated in a concrete way the "universalizing" of ministry in the Church.

Throughout the New Testament, ministry is concerned or associated with *diakonia*—or service—(see 1 Cor 16:15; 2 Cor 3:7–9 as examples). It is associated, too, with special concern for the preservation of teaching and with the preservation of relationships. It is associated with charisms, or special gifts or talents which some individuals in the community have and can use, for the good of others, especially those who can benefit by such talent. For ministry is grounded not so much in the imitation of the historical Jesus as in the personal response to the characteristic call of his Spirit. "Now this Lord is the Spirit, and where the Spirit of the Lord is, there is freedom" (2 Cor 3:17).[9] And, "For as we have many members in one body, and all members have not the same office, we, being many, are one body . . . and every one members one of another. Having these gifts differing . . . (Rom 12:4–8)."

It is especially true that Paul thought of himself as having the charism of preaching, but also of healing and of communication. His "boasting" in the Lord can be seen as an attempt to make clear this very issue: if one has a talent or charism, then one is called to use that charism for others in the service of the reign of God. Without this clear association of ministry with charism and not office in the Church, ministry would be, as Schillebeeckx points out, excessively associated with authority and suffer under the strain of institutionalization. Still, without reference to the need of the community and communion with other believers, it runs the risk of being "violated into fanatacism and pure subjectivity."[10] This is why the "authentic" minister seeks to be part of the believing, worshiping community. Without it, a life-source has been lost.

At heart, notes Cook in his monumental study of the history of ministry in the Church, all ministry is a ministry of reconciliation.[11] The unavoidable responsibility of Christians who see their mission as reconciling the world to the Father and the Father to the world (as Jesus describes himself in John's Gospel) is this ministry of reconciliation, overcoming every form of alienation, of self with self and self with others. As John Shea has stated, pastoral reflection begins when people ask, "What is creative or destructive in their interpersonal lives and systems in which they live."[12] And what is destructive is that which alienates and separates from self, other and God.

Reconciliation: The Ministry of Healing ▪▪

What then is this ministry of reconciliation? Reconciliation assumes several things. It assumes estrangement from a previous or ideal bond or relationship. It assumes that we are meant to be attached, in relationship with one another, with God, with our truer selves. It assumes then an interdependency, but one which keeps us free to develop and grow as we are "called" from birth, to echo O'Meara once again.

Involved in ministry of reconciliation is an overcoming of separations—and healing of those wounds which caused or were received by inevitable separations and loss. These ruptures in relationship can be caused by nature, by sin, by misunderstanding. Jesus' encounter with the woman caught in adultery, the stories of King David, Paul's pleading with the Christians of Corinth and Ephesus, are but some of the countless examples which fill the Scriptures concerning the nature and need for reconciliation.

Ministry, then, is both a restoration of broken bonds and a call to new freedom. Thus, it is directed toward the building up of relationships or community. It is about the business of helping people come together, to overcome the fear that binds them and keeps them away from one another. Healing and binding wounds are paradoxically at the same time a freeing process. The word or communication uttered by the authentic minister is a calling out of bondage, a calling forth to new life—it is the calling forth and unbinding which form the core of the miracle stories of Jesus: "Lazarus, come forth ... Untie him and let him go" (Jn 11:1–44).

St. Paul understood this when he preached freedom from the law. He perceived, writes O'Meara, that the law could not solve the problems of death, meaninglessness and guilt. Law, like fear, its product, is the opposite of freedom from these existential issues. Thus, for Paul it is the Spirit who accomplishes what the law and religion could not. It accomplishes the attachment to a loving God who is eager for it, and the overcoming of the ruptured bonds, the result of sin. The Spirit reveals and works God's universal intention. The "plan of God" which is freedom from guilt, pain and hopelessness, which human beings could not accomplish through a manipulation of the Divine, can now, because of Jesus, be accomplished.[13] It is carried out on the community, in and through others who mirror God's care.

The central problem of life-through-death, which for Paul is at the heart of the redemptive work of Jesus through the cross, involves human beings at the core of existence. This is a "healing of broken bonds" and an example of real freedom. Those who are related to the crucified Christ are characterized by three elements which are inherent in the new status of freedom:

(1) They are spontaneous, and through obedience to Christ, not the law, and a release from guilt are given new lives: God's will constitutes the horizon of obedience, and guilt is now seen as the failure to live up to that to which the personal call of God points.

(2) They are free in spirit and so free from fear, especially the fear of living, changing, growing.

(3) They are free to act responsibly in relationships. For freedom is not a freedom from human entanglements but freedom for healthy involvement. This is the meaning of the baptismal experience about which Paul speaks in Romans (Rom 6:4, 11). It is also the definition of psychic and spiritual health.

To sum up, ministry is the donation of charisms for the service of the kingdom. The kingdom, as a relational reality and not a physical one, is best served when relationships are restored or the ability to form relationships of genuine care is facilitated or renewed.

In their experience, the believers' ministry will undergo the same fate as that of the Master who said that the disciples should not think of themselves as exempt or unworthy of repeating the call to suffering and death. It means then, undergoing—for the sake of the kingdom—attachment, separation and loss in important relationships, with those whom one serves, as well as with one's life. And the one sure attachment and source of strength in any adversity must be the attachment to Jesus himself. "Abide in me, and I in you. As the branch cannot bear fruit by itself, unless it abides in the vine, neither can you, unless you abide in me" (Jn 15:4). This is, in fact, Paul's own experience as a disciple concerned with the ministry of reconciliation.

In an extensive analysis of Paul's relationship with the Corinthian community, Stanley stresses that Paul sought to explain the implications of fellowship and discipleship especially as a healing and maturing reality. "You fail to perceive the body of Christ and so many of you are ailing and sick" (1 Cor 11:30). Paul's concern with the divisive issues (in this case, the eating of sacrificial meat) brought him face to face with a moral dilemma, an issue of conscience, of truth and of charity. Even though he had argued for a freedom from the Hebraic dietary prescriptions, he called for putting a check on the liberty of the strong by demanding submission to a higher commandment of fraternal love for the weak. These weak are in desperate need of a sense of freedom in Christ: it is not a stoic notion of conscience to which he adhered, but rather he saw conscience as governed by charity (Rom. 14:23). And in his Letter to the Romans, Paul further explained that conscience is synonymous with faith.

In 1 and 2 Corinthians, we see Paul interpreting, challenging, offering both acceptance and his own presence. All are aspects of the healing and ministerial function which disciples take on as followers of the crucified Jesus. Individual followers and the community of followers have the same role and function since they have been bonded, united together in Jesus (1 Cor 19:27). To interpret, to challenge, to accept without reservation and to be present are the "methods" of therapy, or the psychic healing process, as well as those of a minister of healing.

Furthermore, we see Paul's own growth pains in the wrestling with the criticisms he faced (1 Cor 1:12–17). He was misunderstood and criticized as being duplicitous, authoritarian and insufficiently present. All these inhibited the bond he thought he had with the community in Corinth.[14] In exercising this mission, Paul realized, right and duty have little to do with effectiveness. Rather, authority and success in exercising one's mission are a direct outgrowth of the ability to stay "connected" to those who are served in love. Authority, he explained in his second letter to the Corinthian community, is derived from the love which one has and develops toward others. Paul experienced healing as he healed, encouragement as he encouraged, and so applied his principles to his own work and the lessons he wished to pass on to his new community. His teaching was a result of his own growth in self-understanding. His effectiveness, then, is a direct outgrowth of the development of identity.

Paul knew loss and failure and felt his own mission and usefulness leaving. He even spoke of being "crushed with heavy burdens beyond my power to bear, so that I even despaired of living" (1 Cor 18:10). He saw this as God's way of forcing the ultimate question: On whose life does one depend? In whom can one put all one's trust? He struggled with oversensitivity, with insensitivity, with being carried away by enthusiasm, and anxiety over having hurt others (Eph 7:8–9, 12–13; 10:9–10). Assessing his own limitations—"I carry this treasure in a clay vessel"—Paul saw death, the ultimate separation from life, at work inside himself. Thus, Paul was able to string together a series of paradoxical insights: In my weakness is your strength; in death I have life; God's strength lies in our failure.

To summarize, then, the lesson for Paul, and by implication for all other disciples, is that maturity in one's mission in life, in coming to mature dependence, arises from the struggle to accept the paradoxical nature of the growth and development process in all relationships. In suffering, separation and loss one is born to new life in relationship, one is reunited to that which is most loved and cherished. This is behind what Paul means when, writing to the Galatians, he states, "You, my friends, were called to be free." We have the courage and ability to act and not simply react because we can never be separated from the love of God despite the ignorance and sin of our lives or the efforts of others to so separate us. For, on God's part, the offer is secure. And, in Jesus, the victory over sin and death has been won.

A theology of human relationship then grew from Paul's personal struggle and his reflection on that struggle as he attempted to "do the will of God" in preaching to the communities at Corinth, Ephesus, Thessalonica and so forth. His letters are a personal sharing of that soul-searching and earnest effort. They chronicle his own maturation "in the Lord."

Toward a Theology of Healing ■ ■

Relatively little has been written specifically on a theology of healing. The psychodynamic process as a healing process has been noted in several works, but a serious examination of the ministry of healing has not. Morton Kelsey, in his monumental study, *Christianity and Healing*, has noted that healing—physical, spiritual and psychic—occurs only "when conditions are right." Physical healing, which is the type of healing Kelsey was most interested in, is "a living process and, as such, is an inner mystery in the end known only to the cells themselves." In other words, Kelsey stressed that the reason some wounds heal—the reason some patients "respond" to treatment on a physical level while some do not—is unknown. Modern medicine and modern psychiatry and psychotherapy cannot predict who will respond favorably, let alone what will work in every instance. They can only describe the conditions most important or necessary for healing to occur.[15]

This notion is stressed in Francis McNutt's work, *Healing*. The inner healing of emotional problems, like the healing of physical wounds, necessitates a "bringing of light" to that which has succumbed to disease in order to allow the Lord to heal and to purify.[16] The Linn brothers in *Healing Life's Hurts* stress the same but emphasize five stages of forgiveness that account for the "conditions" that allow healing to occur. These stages—denial, anger, bargaining, depression and acceptance—follow the stages of dying outlined by Kübler-Ross in her work, *On Children and Death*. The healing of memories, then, is like dying. In this process actual physical healing can occur. Physical healing may, they stress, depend on the spiritual.[17]

Schurlemann, in *Healing and Redemption*, focuses on the human in "isolation," on the brokenness of human life and relationships. He stressed the need for community and continuity in the healing of this "brokenness." The important interrelationship between the physical, spiritual and psychological can be seen in the Scriptures where physical illness has its spiritual dimension. For example, in Matthew 12:9–13 (the story of the withered hand), and in Mark 3:1–5, Jesus noted the way faith and physical healing are related. The ministry of healing, Schurlemann states, is part of the redemptive work of God because sickness is part of or a consequence of the rebellion of humankind and the power of Satan (Lk 13:16; 10:9, 17). Especially in Mark, he notes (Mk 1:23–27, 30–31, 32–34, 40–44), the ministry of Jesus in the area of healing is concerned with casting out, expelling and curing those afflicted by "inner" demons, evil spirits which "know" Jesus in some way. By implication, suggests Schurlemann, there is within these possessed individuals the need to expel or expurgate some aspect or part of their psychic life which is aligned with a destructive, life-stealing reality. Like the leprous, these possessed individuals are outside normal relationship with others. Healing restores their ability to enter into relatedness.

Using a meditation on the Scriptures to inform what is meant by healing, Scanlan in *Inner Healing*[19] focuses on the "intellectual, volitional, affective" part of the human psyche. The mind, will and heart are the sources of emotional, psychic and spiritual malady. Jesus' ministry to healing was concerned more than anything else with this aspect of the human person. Scanlan feels that the Gospel stories of Jesus' healing refer to three categories of cure—physical (e.g., Peter's mother-in-law), the casting out of devils or evil spirits (exorcisms), and the psychical healing which is intended to produce a spiritual or psychic result, as in Luke 5:17–26, the healing of the paralytic. Here, the cure is intended to heal the inner person as well.

When Jesus commissioned the disciples to cure every disease and heal every sickness (Mt 10:7–8; Lk 10:8–9) the intent, then, was that they cure the "inner" as well as the "outer" person. Thus, in various places in the New Testament, the sick are prayed for, anointed, and their sins are forgiven. James 5:13–16 recommends specifically that the sick are to be forgiven; they are to be prayed for and are to be encouraged to respond by sharing their sins with the community. Inner and outer healing are affected at the same time. The link between inner and outer is understood and taken for granted and a third dimension is understood as well—the role of the community. In other words, the effect of illness is to distance, alienate and segregate the person from others with whom he or she is related. The failure to "decide for" such healing is equated with the failure to seek forgiveness for wrongdoing. Tournier, in the *Healing of Persons*, echoes many of these same themes.[20]

This inner and outer tension is reflected in two more important works in the theology of healing. In *Ministry to Deeply Troubled People*,[21] Bruder states that the mentally ill are truly hurt and that these hurts involve deep relationships which have become distorted in some way. In these, the denial of feeling, or the distortion of emotions, common to all, is carried to an extreme because of this hurt. There is, Bruder insists, a wound to the self, a blow to the identity of the person. The loss of selfhood experienced by these individuals is the subject of Kierkegaard's *Concept of Dread*.[22] In this work, Kierkegaard states that the mentally ill are those who have a dread of the good, or that which has to do with the capacity to be oneself, to be free, to be able to choose what is needed for the self.[23]

This interpretation sheds light on the cure of the expulsion of the demoniacs at Gerasene. These demons ask Jesus, "What have we to do with you?" They confront Jesus directly and recognize him as representing the opposite of what they are all about. To Bruder, their sense of guilt, of being cut off from the self and the "God" within the troubled person, is vividly portrayed in the exchange with Jesus: "Have you come here to torment us before the time?" They personify the "feeling of ought-to-be-damned" (Mt 8:28–34).

Finally, Don Browning in *The Moral Context of Pastoral Care* stressed the role of the community in healing and in care.[24] "The major difference," he writes, "between the minister and the secular psychotherapist is that the minister has a direct professional responsibility to help shape the moral universe of values and meanings." In other words, whatever therapy or healing the minister sets out to accomplish, the minister does so within the context of the responsibility to clarify, elucidate and shape meanings and values. These come from the community, the shared faith and hope of the believers within which ministry is carried out. The "community of moral inquiry" is the chief referent for legitimate pastoral ministries.[25]

These reflections on the theology of ministry and the theology of healing, with a cursory examination of the scriptural bases upon which these authors have based their claims, leads to several conclusions. These conclusions give us a tentative handle on a theology of healing which can inform our pastoral reflection and discussion in the chapters ahead.

First, healing as a process is in itself a mystery. Why some respond—whether they be cells or persons—is not immediately known. The unknown, unpredictable, uncontrollable aspect of the offer and the response to it points to the nature of cure as "gift" that is given and received freely.

Second, healing in the Scriptures is considered multi-faceted, or multi-leveled. It appears to be a mix of physical cure, psychic healing, and spiritual healing or rebirth. There seems to be an assumption in the Scriptures that the three are interdependent. This may be close to the truth, as modern medicine seems to be discovering, rather than a lack of sophistication in our medical knowledge of the human person. The concern of Jesus seems equally "distributed." That is, he appeared to be concerned in healing all levels of sickness within a person, even when he was more concerned with the inner reality. Often he cured the physical, knowing that the way to this inner reality would be through a cure of the body. The "issue at stake" in most of the healing stories seems to be the response of the person to the offer of the cure, as in the cure of the man born blind (Jn 9).

Third, whether in the Scriptures or in the study of the therapeutic physical healing sciences, the relationship of the healer to the healed is an important, even crucial element in the healing process. The healer is a mediary of a power or a cure which cannot be equated with him or her. The cure comes from the relationship and the effect of restoring individuals to community, to others. The story of the man born blind in John's Gospel (chapter 9) contains an important additional element, however. In the story, the cure of the individual takes place for his benefit, despite what happens to him vis-à-vis the rest of the community. He is ignored by his parents; he is rejected by the leaders of the people;

and the implication is that he will be put out of the community, the very thing his parents fear for themselves. The relationship with Jesus, then, becomes the focus for the cure—its purpose and result, if you will.

Finally, the ministry of healing involves taking as one's model and tying one's fate and destiny to that of the Master. The disciple or minister can expect, then, to experience the same rejection, the same fears and the same death as that of Jesus. The minister will discover that in healing an important attachment is formed—a relationship with the person in need of healing—and that separation and loss are inevitable. This separation and loss is experienced on the level of relationship and on the intrapersonal level as well. As with Paul (1 and 2 Corinthians), interpretation, challenge, offers of acceptance and physical presence constitute the mode for a ministry of healing.

A Theology of Ministry and Narrative ▪▪

From within several disciplines there appears to be a growing interest in the centrality of narrative. In literary criticism, ethics, theology and psychotherapy, a consensus is emerging on the importance of story as a crucial, necessary and, shall we say, fundamental way of discovering coherence, of achieving a sense of meaning, and for discovering or planting value, especially in matters of suffering, pain and loss. The ethician Alister MacIntire, for example, in *After Virtue,* has described the task of ethics as focusing on how one should live by examining how one has lived.[26] In order to accomplish this one needs to conceive of one's life in terms of a narrative or story. This includes attending to places, conditions, motives of oneself as the subject and author of the story and to others as significant characters within the story.

Although there is a risk of trivialization and miscommunication, the telling and retelling of one's life story is not only the way we come to understand who we are, but it is also the way human beings reach out into the lives (stories) of one another. This is an attempt to create a single story, to be part of some larger, more encompassing story. Some have spoken of this as an attempt to create a common world.

Seen from the point of view of psychotherapy, this task is accomplished when the opportunity is given to grapple in some consistent and sustained effort with the facts or elements of the story. Impressions, beliefs, disappointments, for example, become vital elements in the story even when they might be devalued in day to day living. Seen from the point of view of ministry and healing, the therapeutic situation consists in one individual entering the story of another in order to discover coherence, to embrace all aspects, especially the disinherited and painful aspects of the story, and finally to enter the story as one who participates in the valuing of those good and bad, pleasant and painful elements. The minister of healing is one who willingly risks entering the painful story of another. The Christian minister, moreover, is one who believes that this struggle is not only meaningful but destined for victory and healing.

With the Jesus story as the paradigmatic story of the triumph of good over evil, of victory over death and destruction, the therapist, who senses his or her work as a Christian ministry of healing, embraces the struggle in the client as his or her own. Through this attachment to the client, and through the recognition of the client's uniqueness, the therapist struggles with misunderstanding and rejection and finally loss of someone with whom a great deal of the self of the therapist has been invested. Here the therapist enters into the mystery of salvation. In this, the healing process on both psychic and spiritual levels is accomplished. "Those who are to be raised with Christ must first enter into his suffering and death." To complete our discussion of the narrative process in spiritual and psychic healing we turn to the theology of narrative or story. For this purpose, John Navone's work is especially illuminating and insightful.

A Theology of Story ▪▪

A theology of narrative begins with the assertion that the story is the fundamental way human beings express meaning and values. Story is the vehicle, *par excellence*, for the transmission of our grasp of reality and its significance. Essential to every story is the subject (or subjects) around whom actions, causes and effects take place. "Our life is the search for our own true story with a larger universal story." So, connection with something larger than our own world and our own story is crucial.[27]

Among the many possible starting points for a theology of narration is the story of Jesus, his life and teaching concerning the nature of the kingdom he came to inaugurate. The word, especially in John's Gospel, is the expression of God's own self-understanding in Johannine theology and so Jesus is himself the starting point of a theology of story. The Scriptures, taken as a whole, are a record, or the story of humankind's search for salvation, from various perspectives. They are also the expression of God's passionate attachment to his creation and his efforts at bringing humankind into his story, his life.

"Meaning and values are grasped in images," writes Navone. "Our insights into the true meaning and authentic values occur with respect to some schematic image of concrete expression that serves as a proportionate and appropriate substrate."[28] In order for human beings to grasp the true meaning and authentic values, the power of imagination to represent or create this substrate is necessary. Images, words, symbols and pictures represent to us what is "felt" to be true and gives "flesh" to those less clearly known, unseen, or intangible elements of the story.

Conscious awareness of the meaning and value of events, people and issues is not a requirement for the effectiveness of such things as a story's images. Nor is it necessary that they be current or real. Fantastic past or future events which exist only in potential may have profound impact on us without our conscious realization. The power of imagination is too great to restrict to either conscious or unconscious mind.

Navone insists that the storied character of the Scriptures is indictive of our story-listening and story-telling nature.[29] We learn who we are and what we are through the stories of our cultural and religious heritage. Moreover the uniqueness of the self is also grasped in the recognition of our life as story: I am the only one who can ever be the subject of the story I recognize as uniquely my own.

By listening to this story we become aware of the stories of others, of our interrelationships and interdependencies, for good or for bad. Since the ability to hear a story is the pre-condition for telling one, this skill must be grasped early on. When it stalls, malfunctions, goes awry, then the self cannot heal, repair or discover itself. For to hear a story or to tell a story is to see in it the role one's life plays as center, support, narrator and creator of other stories. As the narrative theologians point out, this implies a potential for transcendence.

Whether in knowledge, in love, or in freedom, to move beyond the particular and finite toward the larger context or horizon (God!) is what is meant by transcendence. This characteristic gives human life its coherence and value. A story's expression points to the transcendental nature of human consciousness. The transcendental structure of human consciousness is given concrete expression in the individual life story as the struggle for meaning and value is engaged. We employ symbols to express and structure our world and in so doing discover ourselves as a symbol of the more fundamental meaning and value which we call God. We are, then, symbolic in our constitution as beings who seek life itself.

Since our story is the only means by which we can interpret social transpersonal reality and the only way that reality can be expressed in its cognitive and affective fullness, the telling of the story and listening to it and to another is the only way we have of living in community. Living in relationship with another demands the continual struggle to appreciate the perspective of another on shared and non-shared elements of the story. A self is known and knows others in their story.

How is all this reflected in the Jesus story? First, the Jesus event is given in four accounts or faces. God's love is manifested as costly in the Markan account. In Matthew's it is fraternal. In Luke's it is universally compassionate. And, in John's, God's love is inhabiting.[30] God is revealed in the four faces of the Gospel story of Jesus. The value and meaning of the life of Jesus is related in the story of his life on earth as one sent to reveal the nature of the love of the Father. Furthermore, like his creation, God's nature is revealed only in the stories of real human lives, beginning with the men and women of the Old Testament, culminating in Jesus and extending to those who believe in him.

Our lives are God-like or are joined with the story of Jesus to the extent that they more or less consciously reflect the same concern of Jesus to do the will of God, to enter the lives of others, especially those in need. His parables, such as that of the good Samaritan, dramatize this very point. Service to others becomes the chief characteristic of the lives of the followers of Jesus. To the extent that we fall short of this ideal of service and selflessness, our story is not in tune with the God story. To the extent that we are unattached, separated, and alienated, we are wounded and wounding, and so in need of a cure.

Finally, the Jesus story is the story of a passionate attachment to a Father as source of life and courage. The purpose of pain, misunderstanding, sin and death is made clear when seen in light of the Jesus event. The completeness and utter desolation of abandonment and loss take on a new meaning. In the life of Jesus these are revealed as potentially redeeming. For rebirth is possible only through a dying—a dying to the things of this world and a dying to self, which means letting go of our efforts at self-protection, self-preservation, self-will and any self-preoccupation which keeps us from attaching to others, especially the wholly Other. The meaning of the Jesus story is seen then from the perspectives of the end of the earthly life of Jesus. The resurrection or rebirth depends on experience of the reality of death. His story, like all human stories, involves both a process (promise) and a completion (fulfillment). These are the conditions for health, life and wholeness, for sanity, sanctity and the ability to experience the self in its fullness by abandoning self-interest.

At least four characteristics of the "storied-character" of our existence are worth noting. The story teller's art is measured by his or her ability to express the complexity of a story. The objective of reflecting on one's life story is to master the details, interpret and give coherence to events, feelings, hopes and fears. These are related in complex ways. Getting the facts right, interpreting them in some coherent fashion, that is, in such a way that they make sense within context, takes work and often guidance, especially when self-esteem has been damaged.

Second, stories are mutual creations. A teller and a listener are needed. In many cases, the listener's role is crucial for helping in the creation of coherence since reflecting back and questioning the story teller's story clarifies the details, the direction and ultimate meanings and values.

Stories have limits. They have a beginning and an end. Without such limits or boundaries the discipline of coming to terms or clarity with events would not be forced on the story teller. The story teller's job is to abstract, that is, literally take out from the flow of life and of events, and illuminate those elements which are significant given the story's end or purpose.

Lastly, stories must express the horizons of the author's vision and are implicit answers to fundamental questions concerning those beliefs, myths, values to which the story teller feels an allegiance or with which he or she has a question. It may be those from whom the story teller feels alienated or those the storyteller is mourning as lost. The stories of attachments from which one must separate require the reimaging of one's life, beliefs, myths, in new terms. The Jesus story, or the story of God's involvement and attachment to humankind, is the paradigmatic story of such a process. Jesus images the Father and in his life story, especially his death, reimages the meaning of life and death for those who accept the challenge of following in his footsteps. His invitation becomes: "Take up your cross to follow me."

This reimaging process has been traditionally called "conversion" because it involves a rethinking and converting of old ways of living, seeing, valuing into newer, more complete images which are more co-extensive with the story of Jesus. It is here that self-surrender and self-transcendence come together.

Thus we have seen that a theology of ministry and healing must stress service and reconciliation of others who feel estranged and cut off from life-giving relationships. Healing involves a response to an offer. The healing of a wounded self must occur within a relationship of genuine care since the wounded self was damaged, or thwarted when care was not forthcoming or denied in some way.

We also saw that this is a two-way street. The healer and the healed as part of one another's story impact one another's self-concept. The healing ministry of therapy occurs or takes place under conditions whereby two people are placing themselves—their selves—at risk. This risk is that a growing attachment may—indeed it will inevitably—result in a painful separation and ultimately a loss.

On the positive side, all experiences of wholeness and value must come as a result of this risk of attachment and self-donation. This "law" of life, if you will, is visible in all relationships of consequence, visible from the beginning of life on in the mother-infant relationship. By risking the completion of the attachment, separation and loss cycle in therapy, the two individuals cross over into healthier, newer ways of relating to important people. Older relationships are clarified and brought into new light. New relationships are possible due to the stronger, more secure self-perception of the healed person.

This somewhat abstract, theological, consideration now needs to be examined from the point of view of the science of psychotherapy. Psychoanalytic psychology and especially Freud's exploration of the subterranean depths of the human mind have had a great deal to say about these issues of attachment, separation and loss. This is the subject of our next chapter.

■ 2 ■

THE ASL-R CYCLE IN PSYCHODYNAMIC THEORY:
The Role of Instincts

Introduction ■ ■

■ Psychodynamic theory, beginning with Freud, has been concerned with the problem of human relatedness, of anxiety and fear, of the reaction to deprivation and loss. What motivates individuals toward, away from or against one another? What causes fear, paralyzes movement and inhibits growth have been major concerns. In fact, Freudian theory and the many variations which have moved away from strict Freudian psychology have nevertheless had to posit a theory of instincts or drives, of motivation and of anxiety. In this chapter we will examine the early treatment of attachment, separation and loss under the headings of motivation, anxiety, drive or instincts. Freud and Bowlby, whose three volume opus is entitled *Attachment and Loss*, introduce us to the parameters of our topic from the psychodynamic perspective. We shall see, moreover, that a too strict adherence to the Freudian version of the nature and role of drives has led to a less than adequate conception of the human person in the light of data on the nature of bonding and attachment.

Effective ministry to those in need of healing means clarifying, interpreting and receiving the life story of one who has been unable to negotiate painful attachments, separations or losses. In this chapter we begin examining human relationships through the psychoanalytic perspective. For this, we need to take seriously the contribution of the early psychoanalysts whose study of motivation, instinct and anxiety inaugurated a scientific and systematic study of human beings in their story.

The Freudian Paradigm ■ ■

Thomas Kuhn has emphasized that any novel conceptual framework is difficult to grasp, especially by those who are long familiar with the previous one.[1] The work of John Bowlby and the branch of psychoanalysis known as the Object Relations School has in the last thirty years produced a conceptual model which more than modifies the psychoanalytic paradigm proposed by Freud.[2] These theorists, especially Bowlby, have taken Freud seriously and recognize that he must be answered directly. This new paradigm begins or rests not on evidence derived from clinical patients in their adult years but rather on childhood traumata and the systematic observation of the normal development of infants and young children.

This model, like any new conceptual framework in psychology, must take account of Freud's seminal contributions, especially those dealing with love relationships, separation anxiety, mourning, defense mechanisms, anger and guilt, depression, emotional detachment, pathology and health, and the important stages of infancy or early childhood. Attachment theorists, object relations theorists and the contributions toward a psychology of self found in the work of Kohut and Guntrip, plus the research of Chodorow and Gilligan, regarding differences in self-perception found in girls and in boys, are more or less consciously based on a fundamental assertion or assumption that there is a natural urge within human beings toward relationship in and for its own sake. This innate drive has self-preservative qualities, but more importantly initiates and fosters the maturation process.

Bowlby began with a metapsychological structure that is psychoanalytic. Later on he moved to his own theoretical framework combining psychoanalytic insights with the data of ethology and the ideas in control and systems theory.[3] His objective: to dispense with drive notions implied in psychoanalysis. Yet, it was not until 1969 that Bowlby offered a systematic presentation of his position beginning with the first of three volumes on "Attachment."

Bowlby has defined attachment as "behavior which results in a person attaining or retaining proximity to some other differentiated or preferred individual." For example, eye contact, touching and establishing a rhythm of interaction—as is done in conversation—are all aids to and aspects of attachment behavior. Crying, calling and attention-getting mechanisms are also part of the repertoire of attachment behavior. This type of behavior is distinct from other "types" such as feeding and sexual behavior, which may also be aspects of attachment behavior—though not necessarily so. The point here is that attachment behavior is a fundamental form of behavior with its own motivation, distinct from feeding and sex, and cannot be reduced to either of these.

As Bowlby has indicated, during the course of healthy development, attachment behavior leads to the development of affectional bonds and "psychological" attachments, initially between child and parent, and later on broaden to include others. Throughout the course of childhood, friendships and other special relationships with important adult figures broaden the child's and later on the teenager's capacity to form relationships with more importance and value to the child than simply the building up of skills or the filling in of "gaps" in developmental areas.

The important thing to note is that attachment bonds continue throughout life and their development is dependent upon the ability of the child to negotiate the nature of the separations and potential losses involved in all relationships. The maintenance of friendships, for example, can be difficult, depending on the ability of the child to plan and execute activity that keeps relationships alive. Of course, the age and the degree of interest and competence are important. No less crucial, however, and perhaps even more important, is the issue of the child's perception of self as both "capable" and "lovable."

In attachment behavior, certain conditions activate the attachment behavioral repertoire no matter what the strength or intactness of the bond. Fatigue, fright, and unresponsiveness, for example, activate it. And this behavioral repertoire may be terminated under certain conditions such as responsiveness from a particular person. When the felt need for care is aroused, then a touch or some such response may be enough to relieve the anxious reaction. This may be totally unrelated to physical needs such as hunger and equally unrelated to sexual or libidinal needs.

Emotions ▪▪

The maintenance or disruption of attachment affectional bonds arouses the strongest emotions. The very formation and maintenance of the bond is called love and the concern over the attachment needs of another is called care. Losing or missing the attachment figure is called sorrow. "Gratification" may be aimed at the sexual or the hunger appetite or at the attachment bond. When gratification is received, anxiety over its absence or anxiety due to possible separation subsides and this is called "contentment." Bonds which are experienced as secure are those which are perceived as unchallenged and stable. Threats arouse anger and unresponsiveness arouses hatred. Renewing bonds is a source of joy. Throughout the ASL-R Cycle affectional states are aroused, and while not all human emotions are directly related to relationships, most are.

Ethology (the study of sub-human species) confirms the fundamental and evolutionary value of the bonding process. Harlow and Harlow in their studies of monkeys have, for example, demonstrated the importance of care-giving figures when experienced as warm and responsive. Contact with warm surrogate monkeys was, for example, more important than feeding from surrogates without a warm surface.[4] For all higher species, risks of danger are minimized and important skills are more easily passed on within the species when attachment bonds are secure. In humans, however, not only are ego skills passed on and id impulses controlled, but a sense of self can develop only in relationships where care dominates.

Care-giving, especially when it provides a sense of security, is a part of all relationships where attachment bonds exist. It is readily seen in the infant-mother bond, but it is a crucial part of all adult relationships as well. It may also be present and visible in the behavior of children toward needy parents. However, a favorable ratio between the weaker, less experienced, and less emotionally secure and the more secure and mature is necessary for healthy development. When older persons depend on children for a great deal of emotional support, then dependencies are bound to develop. In such cases, both individuals stagnate, that is, cannot allow for normal separation and losses to occur, these being too threatening to both the adult and the child. Psychological, spiritual and even physical health depend on proportions approaching equality in dependency and need, as well as in independence and security as the relationships grow. The goal of healthy child-rearing must be, of course, mature relationships of interdependence and freedom.

This has repercussions for how we view a host of behaviors within a relationship. Clinging, attention-getting devices, and anxiety over separation are not signs of regression or "infantile" behavior, since they are bound to accrue in all attachment relationships. Such behaviors become signs of a pathological condition only when they do not develop and mature into more realistic behaviors. Often, such failure is due to unhealthy conditions within the relationship. For example, it is normal for a child or an adult to feel anxious over the absence of an attachment figure when that absence has progressed well beyond its normal duration. With information concerning the whereabouts of the missing person, anxiety ought to decrease, provided the person is old enough to appreciate its meaning. Strong emotional reactions must be in proportion to the degree, extent, duration and realistic possibilities for harm to oneself or the absent figure.

Early experiences influence the attitudes, belief and emotional control involved in attachment issues, as well as separation and loss reactions. Unhealthy reactions can develop in relationships at any stage and the normal cycle in relationships can become "stuck" depending on the experiences of success or failure of those involved in the relationship. It is important to stress, again, that dependency in relationship is a natural part of all relationships. It signals an unmet need or an insecurity in the self of the dependent person. It is as if the other can fill up the gaps, emptiness, and incapacities which the self experiences. New relationships are bound to "uncover" previously unexperienced, unnoticed gaps, or lacks in the self. Therefore, dependency is natural and not an automatic regression, although it could indicate a serious developmental lack or defect.[5]

Attachment cannot be studied in isolation, for attachment behavior which develops naturally leads inevitably to separation—

often experienced as a need for independence on the part of one or both parties. Biologically, the child matures to the point where independence is desired, for example, to test out recently acquired abilities. In the mother, the ability to feed the child, the patience with cleaning and other manifestations of care run their course and independence is expected. When one party initiates separation behavior, anxiety is experienced by both parties. Such anxiety produces behavior which seeks the attachment figure. Protest is bound to develop. Frustration and anger emerge to put a stop to the detaching behavior or, eventually, to give the courage to accept the detaching which is in progress. As a person develops, these "detachings" are easier to cope with and done with less anger and less anxious anticipation. The strength and ambiguity of the bond, not the maturational level of a person, determines the difficulty with which separations are negotiated and losses accepted.

This detaching process signals an end to the old relationship—a termination of the relationships under the previous conditions of dependency. Thus, separation processes lead to real loss and with them mourning. Mourning always involves a self-scrutiny, explained in greater detail in a later section. It is sufficient to say at this point that the self is involved in the detaching and loss process. For the self experiences a kind of death, the death of the former relationship and the conditions on which it existed. This means that the self's understanding of itself must be re-evaluated. A new value (or a devaluing) may be assigned to the attachment figure because of this new appraisal. The same holds true for the self. Once successfully negotiated, that is, once the attachment has produced separation and eventually a loss in relationship, then the self is experienced in a new way. In healthy development, the self knows itself as having survived the process. In other words, despite having lost the relationship under its older characteristics, the self has remained intact, free to go on. It is stronger, even if not less needy of love and care.

Confidence and security and a realistic self-pride accrue in each of these cycles when successfully negotiated. These cycles are important when significant attachment figures are involved, but also occur with less significant figures yielding different kinds of information and building up the self in different ways. For example, when a child experiences its mother as the sole source of nourishment, anxiety accrues each time the mother's absence threatens to interfere with the satiation of hunger as well as when the child begins to experience the threat of her loss as physical presence. A drive for hunger and attachment may not always be clearly differentiated, but are distinct nevertheless. As mother and child progress, mother wishes to stop breast-feeding and the child experiences separation anxiety due to the threat of loss of mother, who is essential for survival.

As progress is made, mother weans the child. Even though the child protests, the child eventually accepts the refusal of the mother to continue feeding through lactation. When the child survives this trauma, as both mother and child learn to live with other sources of feeding, the child is able to reattach to the mother as one capable of feeding through other sources, more independent sources, and is thus able to experience the caring of adults besides the mother. Attachment to the mother as the sole source of feeding, the successful handling of separation anxiety and the acceptance of the loss of the mother as sole source of feeding, in this case, lead to independence *and* a new form of dependency, one which is healthier and more realistic.

Again, this gives the child an experience of self as capable of relating to more than one adult for having needs met. When the separation anxiety is experienced at its most acute level and when real loss and its protest set in, the child has his or her initial experience of the threat of annihilation, and survives when a new attachment, or a reattachment, becomes possible. Self-knowledge and self-satisfaction grow in each of these successfully negotiated ASL-R Cycles. These even grow when the reattachment to the previous attachment figure is not possible, provided that the mourning process has been sufficient and adequate. With significant figures, then, one must speak of dependencies and independencies over the course of the relationship. Increasingly favorable ratios of independent activity over dependent activity are necessary for maturation. Still, some recognition of dependency is equally important for health and maturity. There is then no smooth or single direction in relationship development.

Theory of Motivation, Anxiety and Defenses ▪ ▪

If the goal of attachment behavior is to maintain affectional bonds, then any situation which appears to threaten these bonds will induce anxiety or a reaction of stress. When the threat is acute, it involves the very self as the entity most vulnerable. Loss of the object, if perceived to be permanent in nature, can arouse acute and dangerous levels of anxiety.

In such circumstances, the most powerful forms of attachment behavior become activated—clinging, crying and even angry coercion in infants. Bowlby calls this the phase of angry protest. When the behaviors designed to hold the object of affection in place are successful, the bond is restored and anxiety diminishes. During maturation it is important for the child to experience success at prohibiting a perceived distancing of the caretaker. It is equally important for the child to experience failure. In failure the child experiences the independence of the other and, in such, experiences the autonomy of the self.

Efforts to restore affectional ties are at first constant. Gradually, as a caretaker pulls away or is experienced as "missing," these efforts wane.[6] At increasingly long intervals, the efforts are renewed. Still, the pangs of grief and the urge to search out the lost object can remain primed and under certain conditions become reactivated.

Only late in his writing did Freud advance the view that anxiety arises from a loss or a threat of loss and that defenses are evoked by conditions of intense anxiety. Bowlby has pointed out that the data on very young children indicates that acute distress follows separation, especially when the child is unwillingly separated, when the child is placed in a strange environment, or when care is received from strangers. All these intensify distress despite the satisfaction of other drives, such as hunger.[7]

The sequence of behaviors of a child in such circumstances is identifiable. First, the child protests vigorously, trying by all means available to recover the early bond. Denial, regression to more primitive behaviors—when the child's attachment to mother was secure—phobias and obsessions of all kinds can begin to show themselves. Only gradually, as security is gained, does the child use healthier defenses against anxiety such as sublimation into activities which are positive and ego-building. These might be looked upon as ways of defending the threatened self since loss of the object is a threat to the symbiotically maintained self.

Later on, the child seems to despair. This is especially true when the child is unsuccessful in attempts to restore the bonds. Still, there is a preoccupation with recovery of the lost object and a vigilance for mother's return. Eventually, there is an emotional detachment, an attempt to harden the self to what is perceived as a threat of annihilation of the self. When reunion occurs, reattachment is possible provided the separation and loss have not been too traumatic and some expression of anger is tolerated. Often, the child shows a strong clinging interest in the care-taking figure. The slightest hint of separation will arouse acute anxiety especially when the separation and loss have not been handled or could not be experienced in a "positive" manner. A healthy, positive separation is one which has allowed for reassurance from others whom the child recognized as concerned with his or her welfare. Also it is one where anger is tolerated and where protest has been a successful way to stop separation when the child is not "ready" for such.

In other words, the protest phase raises problems of separation anxiety, despair raises issues of grief and mourning, and detachment concerns the issues of defense mechanisms. While distinct, they are nevertheless aspects of the same single process.

Children are motivated by a desire (or need) to maintain relatedness, for in so doing they can attend to developmental tasks in the security of being cared for and protected. The ability to extend oneself, to risk new activity and to risk oneself in new relationships (as when the child enters the world of school) follows upon the success in maintaining secure, permanent bonds at home.

Defenses in Psychoanalytic Framework ▪▪

Defenses have, for the most part, been treated in piecemeal fashion. Freud, for example, considered repression before advancing a complete theory of defenses. His first paper in 1894 was called "The Neuro-Psychoses of Defense."[8] Grief and separation anxiety were not fully elucidated until *Inhibitions, Symptoms and Anxiety* (1926), although briefly touched upon in *Three Essays on a Theory of Sexuality* (1905) and the *Introductory Lectures* (1917). In *Inhibitions, Symptoms and Anxiety*, Freud wrote: "Missing someone who is loved and longed for is the key to an understanding of anxiety."[9] The best way to understand Freud's mature theory of defenses is to probe the topic of motivation and the nature of the bond between mother and child, the original loving relationship.

The principal features of Freud's model of motivation and anxiety are given in *A Project for a Scientific Psychology.*[10] He states first that in mental functions "something is to be distinguished—a quota of effect or sum of excitation—which possesses all the characteristics of a quantity ... which is capable of increase, diminution, displacement and discharging." Psychic energy, to Freud at this stage, is closely analogous to electric charge.[11]

Reflecting a heavy dependency on Flecher, the Freudian model is governed by two closely related principles, the principle of inertia and the principle of constancy. The first of these concerns the need of the organism to keep mental and physical excitation as low as possible. The second stresses the need to keep excitation constant. "The process of discharge represents the primary function of the nervous system."[12]

Over the years, there were several revisions by Freud especially in the area of anxiety and motivation. The major addition to this theory of motivation is the idea that the principle of inertia can be attributed to the death instinct.

Many authors have since pointed out that Freud's theory of instincts and motivation are direct descendants of the natural sciences, especially the physics and biology of his day. They also point out that Darwin's ideas outlined in *The Origin of Species* have a bearing on Freud's understanding of motivation. Following Darwin, Freud saw instinctive behavior as the outcome of behavioral structures activated under certain conditions and terminated by others. For Freud, the aim of instincts is the cessation of anxiety aroused by chemical and mental disequilibrium. Put another way, instincts seek the pleasure of satisfaction of urges designed to end discomfort and dissatisfaction.

Objects in the environment are soon associated with the satisfaction of urges. The chief object of course is the child's first source of satisfaction, the mother, who attempts to gratify the child's every urge. This then is the origin of "object relations" in the Freudian system. Defenses develop to check impulses which threaten to overwhelm the dissatisfied infant, aiding the ego's development toward autonomy.[13]

Freud and the Mother-Infant Bond ▪▪

Freud's respect for the importance of the mother-infant bond grew during the course of his work. The importance of the mother-infant relationship was not at first recognized. In *The Interpretation of Dreams*, for example, there is a passage in which Freud expressed the view that "when people are absent, children do not miss them with any great intensity; many mothers have learned this to their sorrow."[14] But, by 1926, a serious consideration of the mother-infant bond had replaced these earlier notions. In *Inhibitions, Symptoms and Anxiety*, Freud revised his belief that, apart from a fleeting moment during which the oral component has the mother's breast as an object, all the components of the child's psyche (libido) begin by being auto-erotic. This is the view first proposed in the *Three Essays on Sexuality* (1905) and again was succinctly expressed in an encyclopedia article called "Psycho-analysis," written in 1922.

"In the first instance," he wrote, "the oral component instinct finds satisfaction by attaching itself to the sating of desire for nourishment, and its object is the mother's breast." Freud went on to explain that there is a detaching and growing independence of this auto-erotic drive or focus, which finds an object in the child's own body. Furthermore, other instincts find an external object only after an internal, i.e., auto-erotic one.[15]

Yet, there are in various of Freud's writings, even in the earlier period, indications that Freud believed children to be motivated by more than self-pleasure. In *Three Essays*, again, after referring to the child's sucking at the mother's breast, a prototype of later love relations for Freud, he stated: " ... even after sexual activity has become detached from the taking of nourishment, an important part of this first and most significant of all sexual re-

lations is left over.... All through the period of latency children
learn to feel for other people who help them in their helplessness
and satisfy their needs for love, which is on the model of, and a
continuation of, their relation as sucklings to their nursing
mother...."[16]

Following this statement there is a crucial line whereby
Freud recognized the mutual give-and-take that is at the heart of
this important relationship. He wrote: "A child's intercourse with
anyone responsible for his care affords him an unending source
of sexual excitation and satisfaction from his erotogenic zones."
Freud praised the mother who by touching, stroking, kissing,
rocking, etc., "is only fulfilling her task in teaching the child to
love."[17]

While the object choice is, for Freud, sexual, there is still an
element which is beyond the notion of satisfaction, or pleasure.
In his paper, *On Narcissism* (1914), Freud described these earliest object choices as "anaclitic" because in these early stages sexual instincts find their satisfaction through "leaning up against"
the self-preservative instincts.[18]

Freud did notice, in *Beyond the Pleasure Principle*,[19] that
children become anxious when left alone, and in *Inhibitions,
Symptoms and Anxiety*[20] he stressed the position that the infant
seeks the object because of the satisfaction received. "The situation, then, against which it wants to be safeguarded is that of
non-satisfaction of a growing tension due to need, against which
it is helpless." And "the essence of this danger is of course an economic disturbance caused by an accumulation of amounts of
stimulation which require to be disposed of." The child "dis-
places" its fear from the "economic situation on the condition
which determined that situation, viz., the loss of object."

Finally, in *An Outline of Psycho-analysis*,[21] Freud described
the mother-infant bond as unique, without parallel, established
and unalterable for a lifetime as "the first, strongest love-object
and as the prototype of all later love relations for both sexes."
Love, he tells us, has its origins in the attachment to the satisfaction received in nourishment. Then, he went on to say, because of
the child's inability to distinguish between mother's breast and its
own body, part of the original narcissistic libidinal cathexis is carried over onto the breast as an outside object.

As care-giver, the mother arouses a number of sensations besides those of hunger. Some are pleasurable and some unpleasurable. "By her care of the child's body she becomes the first seducer. In these two relations lies the root of the mother's importance...." This is a reference to the ambivalence played out by the parent from the start and formerly attributed to the period of latency alone. So, by this late date in his writing, Freud was rediscussing the mother-infant bond in terms which his theory of instincts and his two psychic principles could not fully accommodate.

Several writers, such as Bowlby, Jacobson, Greenberg and Mitchell, believe that Freud in his later writings was moving away from the theory of secondary drive. These writers believe he was developing the notion that component instincts have been built into human nature during the course of evolution and underlie the first and unique love relationship, that of mother and infant.[22]

Yet, Anna Freud and other staunch supporters of Freud have later insisted on holding to the position that the mother-infant relationship is built on satisfaction of bodily needs and only secondarily can we speak of the establishment of a relationship between child and object world. Rather, bodily needs and their satisfaction play the decisive role from the beginning.[23] Anna Freud has insisted on what she called "the secondary drive" interpretation. Despite this, in her work with Burlingham, published in 1942,[24] she theorized that attachment to the mother seems to a large degree to be independent of the mother's personal qualities. The potential for attachment is ever-present and ready when the child is starved for an object. In such situations the child will fix on almost anyone. She wrote, too, that the undeveloped and unsatisfied emotions of orphaned children in her study remained latent and "ready to leap into action the moment the slightest opportunity for attachment is offered."[25]

Her paper with Dann in 1951 on six children from a concentration camp experience has been cited by object relations theorists, such as Mahler and others, as evidence of Anna Freud's failure to take complete account of the data received. The positive feelings and exclusive care for one another these children had, even under such harsh conditions, cannot be fully explained as due to the meeting of bodily needs. Rather, the need for attachment alone explains their interdependencies when bodily needs could not be met.

Burlingham and Freud state at one point that the child's needs for early attachment to a mothering figure constitute an "important instinctual need"[26] but they fail to discuss this observation and conclusion within their secondary drive framework. Others such as Melanie Klein, who will be discussed in greater detail in the third chapter, also note what appears to be a primary social bond in the non-oral, social interaction between mother and infant. Still, major emphasis is placed on the needs for food and warmth as biological drives. Nevertheless, Klein is an advocate of the view that there is more to the infant's relationship with mother than the satisfaction of physiological needs. Still, the relationship between food, satisfaction, and feeding patterns is primary. "The study of the fundamental patterns of attitudes towards food seems the best approach to understanding the young infant."[27] Thus, in an effort to remain faithful to the Freudian synthesis, her theory concentrates on orality and on food.

Aware of this emphasis in her theoretical approach and yet conscious of the attachments of the child to good and bad mothering alike, Klein posits a theory of "the good and the bad breast" as the infant's first object relation[28]; she states: "The close bond between a young infant and his mother centers on the relations to her breast."[29] This helps explain ambivalence in key relationships but ties Klein to the theory of instincts and drives which see all attachment and separation behavior as rooted in libido and aggression.

Thus, traditional Freudian theory does not deal with the objects of attachment in such a way that mutuality and interdependence are given priority. Nor does it do so in such a way that the child's attachment or bond with the mother amounts to much more than an instinct for satisfaction of internal (libidinal) drives. The child's seemingly natural drive to seek care and comfort from a relationship with another is relegated to drives for food and for sex, to an instinct for preservation at best. In Freud, drive gratification and discharge of excitation are at times synonymous. It might be said that the basic belief or proposition of Freudian theory is the tendency of the organism to seek an immediate discharge of excitation. Excessive amounts of undischarged excitation can do damage. This is the same as saying that ungratified drives can cause damage. In traditional psychoanalytic theory much of human motivation is reduceable to an effort to avoid this danger.

Likewise, within a strict Freudian paradigm, reality outside the organism constitutes impediments to discharge. Thinking and other complex ego functions such as defenses (conscious and unconscious) are forced into ascendancy due to impossibility of immediate discharge. Commerce with the object world is reluctantly undertaken. If it were not for a delay in gratification, such as the mother's unresponsiveness, thinking would not develop.[30] Even after reality testing and thought develops, the wish must generate the activity within the psyche which initiates the task of drive satisfaction.

As Eagle and others have pointed out, what can be said of thinking (in the Freudian psychoanalytic system) can also be said of an instinctive interest in objects and object relations.[31] An interest in objects would never develop if drive satisfaction was possible. One is forced to posit a "primal hatred" (Freud's phrase) of the object and look for them only as a means for satisfying drives.[32]

A further corollary to this is worth noting. The original narcissistic reluctance to cathect objects is then fundamental and persistent throughout life. As Eagle notes, object investment always entails the potential danger of ego depletion.[33] Self-protection may be natural enough but altruistic drives and the "material" or "care" instinct visible in human interaction are relegated to secondary status. A break from the Freudian paradigm becomes necessary in order to discuss such phenomena in adequate fashion.

Attachment as an Innate Component of the Human Organism ■■

To restate Freud's position on the mother-infant bond: the bases for the child's attachment to the mother lie in the gratification of drives or in the preventing of excessive stimulation which could accrue without an opportunity for discharge. In this way interpersonal attachements have a secondary or derived status. For some, such as Spitz, this position helps explain the clinical data seen in cases of maternal deprivation: the loss of the love object interrupts the discharge of both libidinal and excessive drive. He writes: "I have to stress again that in the emotional intercharge with the love object both the libidinal and the aggressive drives find their discharge. The loss of the love object interrupts the discharge of both drives."[34]

However, ethology and new clinical data show that attachment in higher species of animal and especially in humans appears to be based on autonomous need for what Harlow has called "contact comfort." Harlow, for example, has reasoned that if the satisfaction of primary drives were all that mattered, animals taken from their mothers, as well as infants separated from caretakers, would be "satisfied with surrogates who provide for all necessities." Studies of mental and physical development also reveal the essential requirement of interaction and stimulation by a familiar care figure who is also invested in the welfare of the infant. All temporary substitutes are insufficient, and unable to "induce" growth.[35]

The notion of a necessary "contact" with a caring figure gives a broader vehicle for considering the importance of repertoires of behavior which appear to have no direct link with the satisfaction or release of libidinal or physiological drives. For example, vocalizing, smiling, sucking, soothability, and readiness to respond to certain familiar persons are more readily explained under this broader notion than merely seeing drive satisfaction or orality and feeding, as Klein does, as their instinctual base. Rather, many behaviors make more sense when seen as part of an instinctive or natural attachment for relatedness.

This helps explain as well the phenomenon found in all species where the attachment bond serves important psychological and other survival functions, that is, the feeling of a bond on the part of the maternal figure. The reciprocal nature of the attachment bond itself cannot easily be explained as satisfaction of or gratification of primitive needs in care-giving figures. And the reciprocal nature of the behavior appears to be enough to strengthen the bond.[36] Stern, for example, has summed up the research on the mother-infant bond interaction and believes there is enough evidence now to indicate that relationships are not forged by feeding in comparison to experiential sharing and complementing. He feels that just because satisfaction of certain biological drives, such as hunger, are met by one person, there is no guarantee that subjective intimacy will develop without the accompaniment of subject-object complementarity and sharing (cited by Eagle, p. 37).

In addition, Powell and his cohorts in 1967, plus Silver and Finkelstein, also in 1967, have shown that abnormal physical development as well as psychological and mental development is associated with inadequate maternal attention—despite the satisfaction of physiological needs.[37]

We must conclude that affectional bonds develop due to a primary, natural, instinctive attraction toward a caretaker rather than as a consequence of the gratification of needs alone. The inborn propensity to establish affectional bonds is a better explanation for such observed behaviors as the satisfaction derived from rhythms, patterns, and games played with caretakers, or when visual, tactile, or other kinesthetic stimulation produces delight, recognition and contentment in the infant.[38] It was Balint who proposed in 1937 that "primary object love" is a better way of discussing an infant's early attachment behavior rather than Freud's concept of primary narcissism. And, later on, Fairbairn stressed that "libido is primarily object-seeking rather than pleasure-seeking." Both formulas capture the direction in which the data on attachment seem to point. What, then, is the best way to conceptualize the dynamics of separation and loss, the next two aspects of the developmental cycle?

Separation, Loss and Mourning: Prerequisites for Healthy Development ■■

Anxiety over separation from a maternal figure appears as early as one month after birth, but intense protest and urgent efforts to recover the lost figure emerge at twelve months and can continue for months or years. If the mother does not return, despair sets in, but longing for the lost figure may not cease for years, hope living on in the infant. Restlessness and noisy protests may diminish in time but, with their cessation, apathy and withdrawal from human contacts often follow. The child in such a state is in utter misery.

49

As mentioned earlier, Burlingham and Freud discovered the damage that such a situation can do to the "will to live." Spitz, in 1946, documented this in his film, "Grief: A Period in Infancy," and Robertson has studied grief reactions in children for over twenty-five years. He speaks, for example, of the shattering, overwhelming experience that is the loss of a loved one.[39]

"The mourning responses that are commonly seen in infancy and early childhood bear many of the features which are the hallmark of pathological mourning in the adult."[40] This was Bowlby's conclusion after exhaustive study of the topic. These pathological conditions to which Bowlby refers are four: (1) an unconscious yearning for the lost parent; (2) an unconscious reproach against the lost person, combined with an unconscious and often unrelenting self-reproach; (3) a complulsive caring for others; (4) persistent disbelief that the loss is permanent, a sort of denial reaction.

For mourning to be healthy, then, these conditions must be avoided, and if they emerge—and the work of Kübler-Ross shows that such conditions are quite common and normal as stages of the grieving process—then they must be overcome.[41] The important thing is that grief and mourning reactions to loss must be seen as common and "normal." They become abnormal when the debilitating effects of grief work persist beyond that healthy period of "reappraisal" and stock-taking that separation (if acute) and loss necessarily entail.

Grieving, then, is natural and part of the required psychic processes whenever a loss is encountered. There is important "work" to be done, and in doing such work the self emerges stronger and more secure and better able to reattach to loving or potentially loving persons.

Freud may have set our understanding of this issue back when he proposed that "mourning does not occur in infants." He also wrote that mourning in adults served the one purpose of detaching the survivors' memories and hopes from the dead.[42]

Furthermore, he stressed that hysteria and melancholia are pathological manifestations of mourning following more or less recent bereavement. He likened the experience of loss as having a scar-like effect on the personality and on later psychological development. Such scar-like tissue may form around wounded tissues and lead to more or less severe disfunction in later life if healthy mourning is not accomplished.

What then constitutes healthy mourning? First of all, healthy mourning involves a withdrawal of emotional investment in the lost person over time. This means that a realistic acceptance of the absence and the consequences of the absence of the lost person must be assimilated gradually. Acceptance of oneself as depleted, lessened, impoverished by the loss is also crucial. This is an attitudinal issue which may take time to "accomplish."

Traditional psychoanalytic approaches to the problem have stressed the oral nature of the process of decathecting and the transformation of libido. The painfulness of mourning is accounted for by the persistence of yearning and the sense of guilt and fear of retaliation. This fear of retaliation and sense of guilt come about due to the presence of ambivalent feelings—some of which are aggressive in character—and so arouse feelings of guilt—as if the loss can be directly attributed to such negative hostile feelings.

Mourning is related, then, to anxiety. Freud and Bowlby agree that, as Freud has said in the final pages of *Inhibitions, Symptoms and Anxiety*, when the loved figure is thought to be absent only temporarily, anxiety is bound to result. It serves important purposes such as cueing the organism for reapproaching the attachment figure, a point not stressed by Freud, but one which Bowlby sees as compatible with the Freudian system.

Klein, following Freud, saw fear of annihilation and persecutory anxiety as being primarily involved here. But, fear presupposes hope, for only when we are striving, expecting and hoping for an improvement in the situation are we anxious lest it not materialize. "So farewell hope, and, with hope, farewell fear," wrote John Milton.

Thus, the motivation behind mourning is the regaining of the lost person. This urge is powerful and persistent and not easily related to the reasonableness of gaining the person.[43]

How can we account for the presence of anger and hatred in the mourning process? Again, from *Mourning and Melancholia*, there is ambivalence involved in all significant relationships, so mourning the loss of one is no exception as a process. It is frought with ambivalence as well. Freud did make a distinction, however, that is useful. "Melancholia," he felt, is marked by a determinant that is absent in "normal" mourning, which, if present, transforms the latter into pathological mourning. The loss of a loved object is an excellent opportunity for the ambivalence of love relationships to make itself effective. "Melancholia contains something more than normal mourning . . . the relation to the object is no simple one; it is complicated by the conflict due to ambivalence."[44] So, the more ambivalence, the more difficult the mourning process, which means that difficult relationships are even harder to part with than the less complicated and "smoother," more enjoyable and fulfilling ones.

At the heart of the mourning problem is the issue of identification. Freud saw its presence and significance in both normal and pathological mourning. For the identification issue to be successfully handled, for mourning to proceed in a healthy fashion, then, Freud noted that three conditions are necessary: (1) the presence of hatred must be expressed more or less directly as opposed to indirect unconscious and muted expressions; (2) identification with the lost object is healthy and must be consciously recognized (in *The Ego and the Id*, [1923], Freud seems to have abandoned the theory that identification is always present in pathological mourning but not healthy mourning); (3) finally, in melancholia, Freud stressed that libido withdrawn from the lost object is invested inward, giving rise to a secondary narcissism and a denigration of the self. Healthy mourning will involve a reexamination of the self, a reappraisal of the damages done to the self, and so a certain amount of "inwardness" will be necessary and productive. Whereas for Freud, mourning and melancholia are dichotomous, Bowlby stresses that pathological mourning is simply an exaggeration of these "normal" processes.

But losses are not only grieved in various degrees. There are also different "kinds" of losses which accrue in each person's life. For instance, each important care figure withdraws from the child in order to help the child mature. To the extent that the care figure cannot withdraw and separate, or the extent to which the child is overly anxious and so unable to handle the withdrawal, a child experiences the anxiety of separation, but eventually the loss of the care figure, at least under the old terms of the relationship, becomes a reality. Not only does the child separate and sometimes actually "lose" important care figures, but each time a significant stage of maturation and development occurs, a separation and loss occurs involving the relationship with the care-givers. Although the dynamics of relationship will be discussed in greater detail in the third chapter, it is important to stress here that the child's understanding of himself or herself is bound or bonded with important persons. When growth, or "individuation" (to use Mahler's phrase), occurs, then a rupturing of old bonds will be necessary.

The point here is that the dynamics of mourning, grief, and melancholia (or forms of pathological mourning) are involved in these separation and individuation stages. Ambivalence, withdrawal, anger and hatred at the lost object and the self, guilt, denial, and identification are all elements in the separation and loss cycle whether it concerns the actual loss of the object or the loss of a way of being in the world, or in a movement from one stage to another.

The movement from symbiosis to individuation, from dependence to independence has built within it the aim of mature dependence, healthy independence (another way of saying mature dependence), and the development of the person's full potential. This necessitates a continual negotiation of mourning and loss stages. The depressive position encountered in such a movement, as in other forms of chronic depression, involves the principal problem of helplessness in the face of crumbling or disintegrating affectional bonds.[45]

This disintegration aspect is key. Through a disintegration, the self is taken apart and re-examined. In the process of grieving, the self is reassembled, in time becoming a stronger, more secure self, if the mourning has been successfully done. For, when the self is reintegrated, a significant piece of data has been added as the glue keeping the self intact: the self has been experienced as surviving. When a new relationship of affection is entered into and especially when an old relationship has been re-established on new terms, there is renewed self-certainty, renewed self-respect and additional self-knowledge. The nature and significance of this process and the meaning of the self will be examined more closely in Chapter Five, following a closer scrutiny of the nature of the maturation process itself.

To summarize, Eagle in "Is Grief a Disease?"[46] wrote that the experiences of uncomplicated grief represent a manifest and gross departure from the dynamic state considered representative of health and well-being. It involves suffering and the impairment of the capacity to function, which lasts for days, weeks or longer. We can liken this process, he feels, to the healing process—more so than the disease process. Complete restoration of health is possible, with an even stronger resilience or resistance resulting. Or the process may lead to only partial restoration of former functions or abilities.

This analogy is helpful within the ASL-R model since grief and the process of mourning, like the process of physical restoration of health, is fraught with danger and the possibility of pathology. Something serious has happened to the organism putting the person "to the test." Resources must be mustered and called into action. This is done through self-analysis and self-scrutiny requiring at first detachment, and solitude, and then re-engagement. These are recuperative processes.

As in matters of health and pathology, it is difficult to make a final diagnosis at any one time. What may appear to be a restoration of former functions or former levels of functioning may in fact be hidden increased sensitivity and susceptibility to further trauma. Likewise, what appears as a wound or a scar may indicate a psychological and spiritual strength and depth of character which would not have otherwise existed.

Summary ▪▪

Freud and others have identified the issues and elements of the attachment-separation-loss dynamic in relationship. The Freudian paradigm, however, does not fully account for the innateness of the attachment bonds as a primary instinctual need. Not only does this not account for the data which have emerged in recent studies of infant bonding, but it leaves us with a less-than-satisfying understanding of the human relationship process. Perhaps, this has been due especially to an over-reliance on data from adult memory.

Rather, we need to conceive of relationship as primary and of growth in relationship as a movement toward mature dependency. A cycle of attachment, with inevitable separation and finally loss, leading, hopefully, toward the potential for a healthy reattachment, is the fundamental dynamic for the growth process which accounts for this human bonding phenomenon. Each aspect of this cycle has its own dynamics, first elucidated by Freud, but clarified and expanded by theorists who followed. The contributions of these theorists, many of whom departed from Freud's paradigm, even when they attempted to be faithful to his positions, will be examined in the following chapters.

▪ 3 ▪

HUMAN RELATIONSHIP IN
THE DEVELOPMENTAL PROCESS:
The Contributions of Sullivan and Klein

Introduction ▪▪

▪ The previous chapter outlined Freud's important contribution and the clarifications which Bowlby and others have suggested in the important areas of the nature, scope and direction of drives. We are in a position now to explore in detail the contributions of those who further reformulated Freud's theory, even abandoning it in some cases, however indeliberately. The inescapable reality to those who come after Freud seemed to be the need to account for human relatedness as something more than the satisfaction of a drive toward homeostatis or quiescence. Since our theory of healing in relationship and a ministry of healing requires a sound theoretical framework in psychodynamic theory for its foundation, we now turn to an in-depth look at the psychology of relationships.

An early pioneer in the area of understanding human relationships was the American psychiatrist, Harry Stack Sullivan. His work emphasized the following beliefs. Relationships in humans are a fundamental reality, so fundamental in fact that it can be said humans are known and know others only to the extent that they are in relationship. The human person cannot be said to exist outside of relationship. Furthermore, our needs propel us into relationship and our "selves" are the organizers of the important aspects of our lives-in-relationship. Mental health, then, can be equated with our awareness of the mutuality of our relationships. In a phrase, our lives unfold from the outside in.

Melanie Klein is the perfect complement to Sullivan. A pioneer in the study and treatment of children as well as adults, she approached the issue of relatedness from the opposite direction. For her, the unfolding of psychic life is from the inside out. Where Sullivan stressed the interpsychic nature of human bonding, she stressed the intrapsychic. She accomplished this by placing security on a par with satisfaction when it comes to the nature and direction of human drives. The internal fantasy life of the child becomes the vehicle for carrying the other, the object, and for determining reactions to the outside world.

Both of these theorists made important advances in our understanding of the bonding process, the therapeutic ramifications of which are evident in the way family therapy, for example, has tended to approach the problem of poor and inadequate adjustment. The limitations of this latter therapeutic theory and strategy will also be discussed. However, taken together, Sullivan and Klein highlight the truth that our stories consist of both an internal and an external drama. How well we are able to adjust to the demands of people and things around us depends to a large degree on the early and continuous patterns of relating to key caretakers.

Interpersonal Theory of H.S. Sullivan ▪▪

"Everything that can be found in the human mind has been put there by interpersonal relations," wrote H.S. Sullivan. The only exceptions to this are the capacities to receive and elaborate information and relevant experiences. He went on to say, "This statement is also intended to be the antithesis of any doctrine of human instinct." In this he broke from Freud and strict psychoanalytic theory in a more direct and perhaps more honest way than nearly any other psychodynamic theorist concerned with the nature of object relationships, that is, interpersonal attachments.[1] Sullivan's greatest contribution is to see interpersonal relationships as realities in their own right. In fact, he stressed that when it comes to psychiatry the object of study must always be the interpersonal; the purely personal and individual is a fiction.

With the publication of *Three Essays on a Theory of Sexuality* in 1905, Freud's position on the role of environmental and intrapsychic processes was firmly established. His emphasis on fantasy and interior instinctive drives rather than on the role of the environment as the cause of neurosis remained intact throughout the years, with some modifications to which we have already alluded. It was Sullivan, working apart from the European community dominated by Freud, who attempted to propose a new starting point for the field of psychiatric study and inquiry.

Interpersonal psychoanalysis does not constitute, however, a unified and integral theory as does classical Freudian psychoanalysis. Instead, several important assumptions underlie Sullivan's theoretical approach to the meaning and nature of human behavior and human psychoses. Greenberg and Mitchell have characterized Sullivan's model as a relational/structural one.[2] Along with Fromm, Horney, Thompson, and Frieda Fromm-Reichmann, Sullivan was convinced that classical drive and instinct theory were unable to account for the nature, formation process and difficulties in human relationships. In other words, these theorists believed that Freud did not account sufficiently for social and cultural phenomena.

Background in Clinical Work with Schizophrenics ■ ■

Through his work with schizophrenics, Sullivan was able to determine that an underlying logic and meaning for past and present events is embedded in the patterns of behavior of even the most disturbed people. To him, the fundamental disorder, or "warp," in the psychotic person was largely the result of "a disaster to self-esteem." Reintegrating the self through experiences of healthy relationships is crucial for health since it was in earlier, primary relationships that the person's sense of who and what he or she is had been badly damaged.[3]

Sullivan pointed out that the sexual wishes and conflicts so often a part of the behavior and ideation of disturbed patients are the vehicles for early infantile thoughts and impulses involving dependency longings.[4] This he borrowed from Freud but departed in his emphasis on the role that others play in the building up of poor attachments and difficult separations. He came to criticize Freud for de-emphasizing the importance of relationship processes on the immediate and personal levels, as well as on the social and cultural levels. He referred to Freud's "cultural myopia" as the cause of a "too strict adherence" to concepts like narcissistic neurosis and castration anxiety to explain individual problems.

Sullivan insisted on "letting the data speak for itself." Observable, accessible data—the raw data of observation of those who are suffering from an impaired ability to function in the world with other human beings and to live healthy lives in human relationship ought to be the "stuff" of a scientific psychological theory of human development and mental health. He was always leary of the danger of "reification" of that which cannot be pointed to. In this he was a pragmatist influenced by psychologists such as William James.[5]

Still, Sullivan recognized the necessity of theoretical constructs and built up a theory of psychiatry which assumed that "a personality can never be isolated from the complex of interpersonal relations into which the person lives and has his history."[6] All knowledge and understanding is mediated through interactions. Since personality is a temporal phenomenon and a patterning of experiences over time, the way we know one another is through the medium of interpersonal interactions.

From Whitehead he borrowed his notion of energy as the basic unit or ultimate reality. The "relatively enduring patterns of energy transformations or dynamics" better express what is meant by structures of a psychological, interpersonal phenomenon as opposed to such concepts as "mechanism" or "trait."

Behavior is motivated by two basic forces—the need for human satisfaction and for security. Both operate within the interpersonal field and are bound up with relatedness to others. Under the former, for example, come the simple needs for contact, moving from the infant's need for being held to the more complex needs for intimate relations in adulthood. Because an infant cannot satisfy his or her own needs, human interaction is built into biological requirements for life. Outside of the mother-infant bond, the human infant is inconceivable, he taught. This concept, we shall see, is the starting point for the work of Mahler, Winnicott and object relations theorists. Sullivan stressed this as a lifelong project: "The really highly developed intimacy with another (speaking of the need for the kind of intimacy as evidenced in infancy and adolescence especially) is not the principal business of life, but is, perhaps, the principal source of happiness in life; and one goes on developing in depth of interest and scope of interest, or in both depth and scope, from that time until unhappy retrogressive changes in the organism lead to old age."[7] Depth and scope in human relationships are the developmental "tasks," if you will, of the human-in-relationship.

The human infant's needs are sometimes present at birth, Sullivan taught, but may develop at various times. The need for tenderness (something more than "contact"), he felt, is one such need that emerges after some time and takes various forms throughout life. Each developmental epoch is introduced by the emergence of a need for new kinds or for new levels of intimate relatedness. For example, "need for an audience" is an outgrowth of a need or basic "force" for relatedness. In infancy it is expressed as a desire to have the attention of caretakers. In childhood, it is variously expressed as a need for being competitive, for being cooperative, and for compromise which cooperation entails. In each of these, the "attention" of others to oneself and one's attention to the concerns of others is important.

This develops into the need for collaboration and later on into intimacy with someone of the opposite sex, but only after collaboration and intimacy have been mastered with someone of the same sex. Failure to meet the needs of each epoch results in loneliness and isolation. Following James, Sullivan taught that nothing is so terrifying to the human being as isolation and estrangement.

So, by drawing us into contact and by spurring us to persist in developing our contacts, our needs contribute to the development of a self. From very early on we experience the most satisfying relationships as those which are mutually complementary. Successful negotiation of the requirements of each developmental epoch, then, necessitates complementarity. Satisfaction depends upon this principle.

Sullivan's Understanding of the Role of Anxiety ■■

Difficulties in the interpersonal field produce anxiety and fear. Through what he called "empathic linkage" anxiety is received from and communicated to others. This results in a desire to express needs, bringing us into contact with others, while anxiety itself tends to keep us apart. Often, the caretaker is the un-witting cause of anxiety. This disintegrating tendency cannot be controlled or dissolved easily. Due to the absence of cognitive and other ego skills, an infant is unable to discern the proportions or the meaning and causes of the internal tension which result in being unable to achieve satisfaction. This initiates the separation process.

It was Sullivan who stressed that the infant is unable to de-lineate good from bad experiences and so mixes them into a com-posite picture—a good and bad mother is the first of such composite pictures. Here the mother, as an object in the infant's experience, is discovered as "not completely for my satisfaction." In this, the infant's own self-consciousness emerges. This dawn-ing of self-consciousness comes about naturally, then, from the experience of discriminating two global states—the satisfaction of tensions (good mother) and the increase of tension (bad mother).

At first, these two states are not experienced as referring to a self and an other. The self and the other are fused. It is only later on that the child deciphers first its own reactions and then dis-covers a self in the process. Positive interpersonal integrations build self-esteem, and negative ones, "disintegrations," trigger anxiety and destroy it. Over time, the components of the general integrations are teased apart and the subtleties of parental re-sponses have individual impact on the child's growing awareness of self.

Sullivan's Notion of the Self ▪▪

Greenberg and Mitchell have pointed out that Sullivan's use of the term "self" can be confusing.[8] Sometimes it refers to the content, beliefs, images and ideas generally derived from "re-flected appraisals" which the person contains within. At other times, the self refers to the processes which established and pro-tect the content, a "selecting and organizing activity determining which experiences will be incorporated into the self."[9] It is suffi-cient to say that both notions are important in Sullivan's theoret-ical formulations. Not until much later on, in the work of theorists and clinicians like Kohut, Guntrip and others, does the notion of self become a clear and well-defined concept in psychoanalytic thought. (This discussion will be taken up in Chapter Five.) In general, Sullivan was concerned to highlight the "sentiment of self-regard," the self as organizer of experiences, and the content of the self, and when so doing he delineated which aspect of the self he intended to examine. How does the self-system, then, emerge?

The experience of the good mother and the bad mother has its correlate in the self-references of the child. The good me and the bad me develops in the child and constellates the complex organization of experiences deriving from interpersonal relationships with key individuals. These are the "reflected appraisals," the opinions, feelings and attitudes of others about the self. A self-system then develops to keep anxiety at bay, especially anxiety of overwhelming proportions.

The term "self-system" refers in Sullivan's work to the functional, operational aspects of the self. Representational aspects of the self—what I think I look like to others—were later called self-personifications. It is the goal of the self then to reduce anxiety and to present a person who meets the expectations of significant others. In so doing, the child begins to separate from, and then evaluate, not only the actions and attitudes of others who are important but also to evaluate and discern his or her own attitudes, values, and actions. There is in the process of "separating out" an anxiety over the emergence of a self which is distinct and under evaluation, both by others and by oneself. Yet it was Klein who studied directly the infant's and child's anxiety and who better described the role that anxiety plays in the generation of self-concepts. For these concepts are able to carry the individual in relationships as needs for satisfaction and security are being met.

Summary ■■

Although Freud was the first to note the importance of familial dynamics in the development of the child's intrapsychic life, it rested with theorists such as Sullivan and Klein to study and elaborate how familial, social, cultural, and environmental factors influence normal and abnormal personality development. Sullivan abandoned the linear, mechanistic theory of the libido and viewed the personality as developing out of interpersonal relations with parents, peers and the wider culture. The self then is a reflection of interpersonal relations and, as such, is not a static entity but a process. Mental health, for Sullivan, can be equated with the awareness and "health" of one's interpersonal relations. This approach has had a great impact on general systems theory and on family relations theory which will be examined in the last section of this chapter. For now, it will be helpful to explore in greater detail what Melanie Klein has contributed to our understanding of the "internal" side of our social nature. The need for satisfaction and the need for security in all children is the source of anxiety forcing the child to conceive of a separate self. For Sullivan, there is also a tension between these two basic needs. The pursuit of satisfaction may interfere with the pursuit of security since the effect that the child's pursuit of satisfaction has on mother is often a negative one. The demands of the child amount to an infringement on her freedom and mobility. She also knows that the infant needs to become independent so as to learn to satisfy itself and be less dependent on her.

It is the pursuit of security that leads inevitably to problems in human relationships. However, since "any interpersonal situation is prone to stir conflict between the drive to re-affirm the importance of the self and some other drive for satisfaction by way of cooperation, the pursuit of security, if unchecked, crowds out the pursuit of satisfaction. Prestige, status and the way other feelings tend to dominate awareness."[10]

Melanie Klein and the Intrapsychic Life of the Child ■■

Klein had a very different perspective on the infant's development and satisfaction of needs but one which is complementary to that of Sullivan. To her, the infant's life unfolds not from the outside inward, but from the inside outward. In this she was closer to Freud. Internally arising object relations emerge, clash, are blocked, channelled, or contained by social reality. Her focus was on object relations from an intrapsychic viewpoint, whereas Sullivan's was on the interpsychic. An interpretation of Freud suggested by Guntrip helps clarify Klein's position vis-à-vis orthodox psychoanalytic thought.

Background in Freud ■■

In his analysis of Freud, Guntrip concluded that Freud's ideas fall into two main camps: those which concern the id-ego-super-ego, or id-plus-ego control apparatus, and those surrounding the Oedipus complex of family object relations. These latter are especially important, for they reappear in the treatment process as transference and resistance, a subject which will be taken up in the discussion of particular cases of therapy with children and their families. The first group of ideas utilizes the laws of physics which prevailed in Freud's day and are the source of much criticism that Freud's notions are mechanistic and impersonal. As we have seen, his theory of homeostasis and the process for reducing the tension of disequilibrium does lend itself to such a charge.[11]

In his ideas regarding the nature of human relatedness Freud was more concerned to explain how human beings affect one another's psychic life. Here he left the idea of sex as an exclusive energy and began speaking more of the role of aggression with its obvious social concomitants of guilt and depression. For the overcoming of the complex, identification and repression are key accomplishments. The superego's development, less biologically based than the id or ego, is where Melanie Klein began her own formulations and inquiry.

Klein intuited that the pleasure or constancy principle may be a valuable way of describing the functioning of the organism but can be misleading when applied to the way important relationships work. By focusing on the object relations of the infant, Klein felt that she was developing the core of Freud's ideas, with less emphasis on the psychophysiological. To do so, she studied the mental life of children directly, something which Freud did not do. Her supporters feel that her focus on the role of the mother in the child's internal fantasy life balances Freud's focus on that of the father.

Klein described the struggle between the forces of love and hate (Eros and Thanatos) in dynamic, internal terminology. She accorded the death instinct the larger role of the two. By doing so, the forces of death tend to cloud the picture of child development. This renders her theory difficult to understand or accept in places.

The child's negative and persecutory feelings are given heightened significance. And her analysis of anxiety as the contributor to and result of aggression and thanatos is not subtle enough for most theorists today.

Role of Internal Fantasy ■■

It is the internal fantasy life of the child, nevertheless, which is the seat of emotion-laden notions that accrue from relations with objects, especially with the mother. Kleinian instincts are primitive forces locked inside the child's nature. The first love object, however, is the child's own primitive ego. This she calls the state of "primary narcissism." The child becomes attached to its first external object through a process of projecting its self-destructive wishes onto the "bad breast" or that aspect of the mother (outside reality) which does not or cannot meet the needs for satisfaction.

External objects, then, are valued, not as objects in themselves but rather as receptacles for the child's projection. Through this process an inner world of fantasy develops which is "object relational." It is the counterpart of what takes place in the ego as it relates to the world of real objects—all centered, for the most part, around the mother. At the core then of Kleinian theory is the notion of projection and introjection. These are the result of the fact that the infant must live in both an internal and an external world. In normal development the external world comes to dominate more and more. Through this sort of analysis, Klein shifted the discussion of the infant's psychic life from the image of a "seething cauldron of instincts" (Freud's phrase) to that of a personal world of object relations. These object relations are first expressed in the child's fantasy life, even before pictured or thought, and are finally the work of the child's growing ego and self.

This focus on the "person-ego in object relations," as Guntrip sees it, is reflected again in her approach to stages of maturation.[12] Where Freud postulated an oral, anal, phallic, and genital series determined to a large extent by psychobiological factors within the child, Klein's emphasis shifted to a look at what she called the two fundamental "positions" vis-à-vis object relations. These reach across stages as the child must interact with important care-takers. She called these phase the depressive and the paranoid-schizoid positions.[13]

The essence of the depressive position concerns the need to master persecutory feelings. Klein held that in the second quarter of the first year of life the infant begins internalizing the whole object—not simply aspects of the mother. In this, the infant is forced to integrate the good and bad aspects, or objects, which were features of the mother. Destroying the bad mother would also involve destroying the good mother, producing horror, dread and fright.

On the other hand, the paranoid position and the anxiety it produces involves a fear of being destroyed by outside objects. The difference between the depressive position and the paranoid position's anxiety is that the depressive position involves a fear of destroying both good and bad objects. Through reparation, the child hopes to resolve guilt and anxiety. This is done through re-storative fantasies and behavior.[14]

Focus on Love and Reparation ■ ■

Thus Klein insisted that the child's authentic love and grati-tude for the mother begins at the breast and achieves a central focus when the child introjects the whole object in this period of four to six months of age.[15] The depressive position is important because it results in the infant's appreciation of the object as "other" with whom the infant feels intensely and intimately re-lated.[16] For Klein, this depressive position takes precedence over the Oedipus complex because it involves the very possibilities for relationship.

By shifting our focus toward the importance of infantile fan-tasy life and the relationship with mother, the importance of life-long conflictual feelings becomes clear. All loss, then, contains an element of those feelings that one's destructiveness ideation has played a role. This further explains why a child may interpret a loss as a retaliation for hatefulness and past injuries.

Klein helps us appreciate an aspect of the separation and loss process in her explanation of the depressive and paranoid posi-tions. These lead inevitably to and are the result of feelings of estrangement and individuation since they produce and result from the realization that mother cannot be controlled; she is not me, and cannot be completely "for me." In the loss of the mother due to the failure to get her on the infant's own terms, the infant experiences depletion, desolation, and the diminution of the capacity to create and control without accounting for the needs and feelings of others. These feelings are a necessary and important part of all relationships which constitute our interpersonal life.

Good experiences in key relationships, of course, have an important and necessary effect, one to which Klein does not refer enough. Good interpersonal relations augment the belief that one can use one's power and one's abilities to love and influence, to repair damages in relationship done in frustration, anger or hate. When one has been forgiven and when hate and anger have been checked, the infant experiences both self-control and the independent status of the other. The child's own sense of self, bound up with important others, is enriched since it is given importance and status as a truly creative agency.

When Klein insisted in a rather heavy-handed and potentially confusing way that "the infantile depressive position is the central position in the child's development," she moved psychodynamic theory into a different light. The focus is now on love and reparation in human relationships and not on jealousy and guilt.[17]

It is also useful to point out the important contribution Klein made in her focus on envy. To her, envy is rooted in the presupposition of a constitutional aggression. She proposed that envy is best understood as a product of innate aggressive forces directed toward the good object. The child experiences the goodness and nurturance of the mother but resents her control and her power over the timing and quantity of her care. Intense and greedy needfulness and dependency on anxious and inconsistent care-takers combine with the infant's inability to conceptualize the reason demands cannot be met. Thus early aggression is unavoidable. In this way, we can understand the important, built-in factors motivating the child toward independence, spurring the separation and individuation process.

Thus, hatred and envy, from wanting more intense and complete care, lead to inevitable splitting and spoiling in the relationship with the mother. Ambivalence pervades all important relationships. And, due to ambivalence, the struggle to understand the other and the self in relationship is intensified. Splitting, projective identification and ambivalence are three concepts which family relations theorists have taken to help explain intrapsychic processes involved in interpersonal relationships.

Because of her strict adherence to Freud and descriptions of the child's inner life which are sometimes difficult to follow, Klein may be hard to accept without nuance, reservation and qualification. Relegating emotional energies to libido and aggression does not, moreover, seem consistent with her notion of the primacy of object relations. Still, her shift of focus on the directional quality of drives implies that drives are not only attached to tension-reducing stimuli but have the object as a constituent element in their nature. They are longings aimed at specific eidetic images. It is not clear that Klein has been able to describe the fundamental organization of object relations and emotional life and preserve at the same time the notion that all significant constituents of mental life are internally given.[18]

For Klein has not adequately accounted for, first, the structures which are needed for images to be present (internal or external), next the drives as they are absorbed and brought to bear on internal fantasies, or finally the way experiences merge and organize themselves. Object relations theorists who will be presented in the next chapter, specifically Mahler, Fairbairn and Winnicott, have given a more complete account of how the phenomenology of experience is organized into personality and the maturation process.

Family Relations Theory and the Contributions of Sullivan and Klein ■■

Since key interpersonal dynamics take place within a family, it might be helpful to examine the theory and practice of family relations specialists. The influence of both Klein and Sullivan on Jackson, Lange and Slipp has been enormous. This branch of theory and therapy has contributed a great deal to our understanding and, with recent developments in family therapy and system theory, have a great deal to contribute to our understanding of the way relationships function in the family unit.

Donald Jackson, one of the founders of the family therapy movement in the United States, became dissatisfied with traditional psychoanalysis because it could not adequately account for the way family interactions protected, nourished and generated emotional disorders in some patients.[19] To Jackson, emotional dysfunction is primarily the outcome of family interactions. Pathology, he believed, exists only in relationship. In this, his work borrowed directly from Sullivan. Jackson also developed, from cybernetics and systems theory, the notion of the feedback loop.

Gregory Bateson is perhaps more helpful than Jackson in stressing that systems theory reminds us there are at least three subsystems present before the therapist: the individual must be seen as a system in himself or herself; the interpersonal relationships of the individual form systems of which the therapeutic relationship is one; finally, the family as a whole is a system. All of these systems, moreover, are interacting.[20]

With Melanie Klein's focus on the child's internal object relations in mind, we can see object relationships as a theoretical "bridge," as Slipp has called it, between individual and family theory and treatment. Object relations, claims Slipp, helps to indicate "the fit of the individual into the family system and the effect of the individual on the system."[21] By its focus on attachment and differentiation within the family, object relations theory has given family therapy a way of assessing the internal dynamic process in unhealthy family constellations.

Family systems theory has forced us to respect the fact that individuals, especially children, must live with other people who are powerful influences. Klein and others have helped us see that these significant other people live "inside the child" and so are present in some manner during the course of therapy. Second, family systems theory has stressed that the therapist, by helping one person, is in effect influencing a system. By modifying the behavior of one person or influencing the self-esteem of one, the entire configuration and manner of interpersonal dealings will be affected. Robert Lange has stressed this in his concept, the "bipersonal field" in therapy, as it influences other important systems in the patient's life.[22] This interest, however, is not new, nor are these ideas recent discoveries.

Within the early psychoanalytic circles, it was Sandor Fer-

enczi who first discussed these issues after examining the problem of parental neglect. His clinical practice concentrated on the
dependency needs of adults and children. He stressed the concept
of developmental arrest, a result of parental neglect, and believed
that, if the therapist was emotionally available, warm and empathic, the patient would be able to regress to the time of the unfulfilled dependency need. Freud feared the potential for over-
involvement with patients (as in the Anna O. case). Countertransference feelings become the key, in Ferenczi's mind, for exploring
these needs, especially with the sicker patients.[23] It was Ferenczi
who first stressed the patient's projection of internal fantasies
onto the analyst and onto others as a way of using these persons
to fulfill unmet needs. In this sense he may be the first "object
relations theorist."[24]

Fantasy life of the child is a crucial concept in the work of
Freud and Klein. However, Ferenczi's approach, like Klein's, differs in a significant way from Freud's. To Freud, instincts create
fantasies, and to Ferenczi and Klein it is a child's fantasies which
produce instinctive reactions.[25] It is, as we have seen, by and
through fantasy that the infant splits experiences into pleasurable
and displeasurable ones according to the pleasure principle.
These ideas have relevance for family therapists.

Projective Identification ▪▪

Family systems theory and research has shown that the fantasy life of the child has enormous effect on the course of development of the family system. The child's fantasy life is often
reinforced by external reality, which the child helps create.
Through projective identification the child attempts to control
and return to the mother and in controlling her seeks to make her
the good mother or the bad mother, avoiding the difficult process
of incorporating ambivalences and nuances.[26]

If the child's fantasy or belief is unhealthy, and if something
in the family or system supports or confirms this belief, the child
becomes fixated at this point of development. The child, then, is
"stuck" in a faulty interpretation of reality. For example, if the
child fantasizes that the mother cannot get by without attachment

which is presently in effect, the dependency state becomes fixed. The mother's anxiety about separation and differentiation reinforces the child's hesitance and solidifies the belief that the two, in fact, cannot afford to separate. This "system" functions intact until something outside it, school for example, intrudes into the world of the anxious mother and the over-dependent child.

Another "systems" example may be a family which fears aggression and competition—usually because these have been poorly negotiated by one or both parents in their own childhood (their own fixation point). The child begins to believe that omnipotence fantasies about destructiveness in aggression and competition are powerful and able, in fact, to destroy the family. When the child cannot complete or express aggression in the home or family, he or she may take these now powerful feelings to another arena, the school, for instance, where they may be sublimated into healthy competition or emerge in an unhealthy fashion. Examples of how beliefs and fantasies of children, as they grow out of and create reality in the family system and affect other worlds in which they live, will be further examined in the clinical case material later on.

This process whereby information confirms a negative situation and reinforces the child's perception of reality and self has been called in family systems theory a "negative feedback loop." It is a reinforced, unhealthy belief. In other words, supporting data for the child's unhealthy version of reality is generated by the manner in which the child relates to and attempts to control the behavior of significant others. Significant others "support" this inhibiting situation unconsciously.

As the child matures socially and physically, relationships are "set up" to support the particular belief or style. This assumes fluid ego boundaries and a poor sense of self, or poor self-esteem. Several patterns of family interactions have been identified when splitting and projective identification have been employed in an unhealthy manner, fixing the child at an immature developmental point. The inability to differentiate self from others, known as the symbiotic survival pattern (seen dramatically in cases of schizophrenia); the "double bind on achievement" pattern (seen in most depressions); a pattern of prevented separation and individuation or the seductive binding pattern (seen in hysterics and borderline patients); the pattern found in delinquency where the child in anger must rebel to assert a negative identity: all four are identified by Slipp as developing when self-object differentiation and separation are not responded to in an appropriate manner by parents.

This represents an important set of contributions to ASL-R Cycle model. Children who are "enmeshed," to use Minuchin's term, within such a system do not mature. That is, they do not become individuals who are able to express needs and other legitimate claims for affection on parents. They cannot pass through difficult waters of maturation. There are tendencies within and outside the child, in the child's family, which may be threatened by authentic separation and loss. In therapy, the therapist becomes one of those with whom the child becomes attached, must separate from and finally lose, and so the fixation point is bound to emerge and become "visible" during the course of therapy in the transference and countertransference.

Slipp and others, building on Sullivan and Klein, have contributed a great deal to this concept of projective identification which is so important in family systems theory and therapy. The key aspects of this concept can be summarized as follows: (1) projective identification functions as a primitive intrapsychic form of adaptation and defense based on fantasy and is normally used during infancy; (2) it is a form of interpersonal defense to sustain the family's integrity, as in the symbolic survival pattern; (3) it is a form of object relations in which one lives through the other; (4) it is a method of manipulation and control based on omnipotence fantasies; (5) it is a form of communication designed to induce a response; (6) it is a method of ridding the self of certain aspects and inducing pathology—negative response patterns in others; (7) it is the source of the organizing of negative feedback loops, originating (or fixating) in development; (8) it may be the source of what Winnicott called the "objective" countertransference in therapy. That is, as the therapist begins feeling "sucked into" the patient's reality and fantasy, he or she experiences the actual problem, i.e., sees it first hand.

One final advantage of the concept of projective identification may be its usefulness in understanding the artistic productions of children during the course of therapy. This can be seen in the artistic productions within the therapeutic process. It will be sufficient to say now that children in communicating with their therapist and with their own psychic processes project their identifications and the objects of their fantasy life onto or "into" their own productions. They do this to examine them in the safety of the therapeutic environment. For the therapeutic environment, as a holding environment, is able to support the scrutiny of fantasies and beliefs when the environment is not punitive should the fantasy not stand up to the test of reality. It must be one where the therapist can actively use the projective indentifications, gently exposing them and opening them to scrutiny. This is due to the nature of transference and countertransference processes.

Finally, family systems theory has also contributed the concept of family homeostasis, an interpersonal interpretation of the Freudian concept of the organism's tendency to achieve or seek out equilibrium. In interpersonal and systems terms, this refers to the transference and countertransference balance that becomes permanently established between spouses as, for example, they unconsciously collude to regulate a negative feedback loop in relationship.

This serves them to perpetuate a pathological cycle of interrelating. A husband whose self-esteem has been poorly established is not sufficiently strong to withstand damaging evaluations in the workplace, and so may manipulate his wife (as a way of feeling superior) into positions of failure. Realizing that these failures serve a "valuable" function, she may continue the "fantasy" of her own inferiority. As a way of exerting her own superiority, she may later on bring the child into collusion with either herself or her husband. This may give her a forum for her own and/or his fantasy. In family systems terms this is known as "triangulation." In Kleinan terminology, the child's defensive splitting, of the good and bad parts of the family situation, are internalized. The good and bad parts of the self tend to become triangulated into the relationship or interaction. In other words, the internalized object world of one or both or all three persons is projected into the external, marital or family relationship. In the marriage, old conflicted relationships are acted out, resurrected, and recapitulated in the marital relationship. These are further displayed in the relationships with the child.

Sometimes, when the child reaches a stage or developmental epoch in which a parent had difficulties, the parent communicates his or her own unresolved conflicts and these are "resurrected" in the interactions with the child. So when parents have had difficulty negotiating attachments, separations and coming to terms with losses in their own childhood, they are likely to become overly anxious when their child reaches a stage where similar difficulties arise, feeling helpless and vulnerable, as old wounds are exposed. Thus the parents are likely, in an unconscious manner, to foster pathological responses in the child. (Sullivan's term is "empathic linkage.") The child then accepts as part of the self the projective identifications of the parent. Placing them inside, they become part and parcel of the internal object world (Klein).

Limitations of Family Systems Theory and Family Therapy Model ▪▪

The question arises: If an object relations approach to family systems gives a clearer indication of the interpersonal and the intrapsychic processes, then would an integrated theory (object relations, interpersonal relations and family systems theory combined) give us the best model for therapy with children and families, especially if that model assumes the attachment, separation and loss dynamic? There are several limitations to a wholesale adoption of family systems theory with regard to a pastoral model for work with children and their families.

First, while role-playing, negative feedback loops and projective identifications exist in all families, there is a tendency in family systems theory to see the family as having the problem and that the problem can be dealt with by examining present behavior and patterns of interaction.[27] It is true that in many cases the child or one member "takes on" the neurosis of the family and becomes the "victim." However, often these individuals are not available for therapy, or are unwilling to be in therapy. In cases of divorce, for instance, an important person is often not able to be present for a variety of reasons. Thus, the family therapy model may not be "workable" in many instances. The "pastoral" therapist accepts whoever seeks therapy as worthy of assistance no matter who cooperates.

Secondly, a focus on the pathology within the family system may mislead the therapist in some cases. Difficult to accept separations and losses, as in the case of the death of a parent, mean that the difficulty is not best conceived in terms of a family systems neurosis or pathology. In working with children, because of their vulnerability and powerlessness, focusing on the healing of memories, the enactment of successful attachments and separations in therapy provides a better approach fitting a wider variety of cases, not just those where the family system has contributed to or created the neurotic behavior of one family member.[28] Often, by coaxing the parents into working for the child's improvement and changes in behavior, the therapist may allow the parent to believe the child has the problem. When the parents believe that their work and that of the therapist is having an effect, they are in fact allowing for changes in the system, breaking negative feedback loops.

Finally, because children are vulnerable, because ego boundaries are fluid, and because the self is fragile, these ego boundaries need to be protected and the injured or thwarted self needs to be nurtured. In settings where other family members compete for the attention and affection of the therapist, the therapist must become problem-centered instead of person-centered. This is especially problematic in cases with vulnerable children. Healing and nurturing cannot go on when the therapist's interest is constantly focused on the family system or family problem. The privacy and uniqueness of the relationship with therapist and child may be crucial for the healing of the self, without which the child would remain fixated at a particular point in the ASL-R cycle.

This points to the need to examine further the theories of maturation and development, especially those which focus on the attachment, separation and loss process. It will also be useful to examine the growth and development of self-esteem. These two areas of study, which complete our theoretical analysis, lay the foundation for seeing the therapeutic process as concerned with issues of attachment, separation and loss. As a healing relationship, the therapeutic relationship revolves around the same three dynamic processes. The self is healed through this cyclic process.

Conclusions ■■

By drawing attention to the negative effect on the mother which the child's security needs produce, Klein was able to account for the ambivalence, envy and rage which relationships of importance produce. She was able to take the issues of anger, jealousy and guilt back to even earlier periods in the child's life, to the first year of life, in fact. This makes them appear more fundamental, more innate than they do in Freud's work. The gradual reduction of grandiosity in the feeling of powerlessness and helplessness over the mother explains the increasing realism of the child.

Klein and Sullivan speak of feelings—envy, hate, joy, worry, and so on—and so move us in the direction of a less clinical, less scientific (in the narrow sense of the term) analysis of the psychic life of children. And by using such terms as "position" instead of stage, Klein was able to move away from an emphasis on distinct periods and toward the direction of seeing the recurrence of issues and problems throughout the life cycle. This movement from a psychobiological emphasis to a concern with emotions as opposed to drives helped lead the way for a more courageous break from Freud by later theorists.

Most important, Klein was able to introduce topics of guilt and reparation as important elements in all relationships and as fundamental to the bonding process. She did so outside of the exclusive umbrella of libido, or sexual energy. Fearing that mother's unavailability and absence are caused by excessive demands, the infant, she hypothesized, seeks to restore the bond through appeasement, a definite turn toward the other. Even if done with selfish interests at heart, the turn is away from the self and so cannot be completely explained in "sexual" terminology.

Family systems theory from a pschodynamic perspective has attempted to combine the interpsychic and intrapsychic ideas of both Sullivan and Klein. While it is true that the child is a system involved with other systems and that to affect one member of the system is to have an impact on all members of the system, there are limitations to a strict family therapy approach. Such an approach may give priority to "the problem," not individuals, without intending to do so. For example, when an attempt is made to understand the difficulties occurring in the family, it is important that each member of the family be able to "tell the story" as he or she sees it.

In the case of children, the unfolding of the story, the child's interpretation and understanding of events, may emerge in ways other than with language. If language is the chief vehicle of therapy, the child's story is likely to be buried. When adults "name" and interpret events first, children are often too unsure and too weak at renaming, retelling and reinterpreting from a different, i.e., their original, perspective. Often they assume that it must be the way mom, dad, or an older sibling described it.

Finally, children and individual family members need the special attention of one who is concerned more with their individuality than with the issues and problems which they face in the family. A conjoint family therapy approach, for example, may not easily fit within the ideas of the healing and therapeutic process described here. Competing realities need not only their day in court, but also the acceptance and respect they deserve as the "story" of an important participant.

THE DEVELOPMENTAL CYCLE IN OBJECT RELATIONS THEORY:

The Contributions of Mahler, Winnicott and Fairbairn

Introduction and Overview ■■

■ Because of a very different methodology, Mahler and her cohorts, plus Winnicott, have avoided some of the problems and pitfalls mentioned in the discussion of Freud, Sullivan and Klein. The object relations theorists whom we will examine in this chapter have studied mothers and children, and in some cases fathers as well, in other than a strict clinical setting. Often these theories grew out of observations of infants with their mothers in natural settings without intrusions of foreign persons likely to affect the dispostion of the child. Yet, these theoretical formulations presume the foundation laid by Sullivan and Klein.

For Margaret Mahler, the role of important others, especially the mother, results in making self-integrity and independence possible. Maturation takes place when the mother is internalized, that is, becomes an object existing on the "inside" as well as existing in the real world. For healthy development, the child must be able to experience a psychological independence from her which conforms to a realistic, or age-appropriate, sense of autonomy. The ability to become independent of the mother develops when the mother is carried on the inside. Over time, a gradually expanding orbit of important care-giving relationships (first mom, then dad, then siblings, grandparents, peers, etc.) develops from the healthy attachment bond which not only tolerated, but encouraged, independence and self-expression.

Winnicott prefers the term "interaction" to condense both intrapsychic and interpsychic processes. His discussions of the importance of "the illusion of omnipotent control," the mother's necessary and useful failure, and the concept of good-enough mothering are helpful and appealing. They take the burden off of what may appear at times as an impossible parenting task when it comes to producing children with adequate mental health and normal self-esteem. Both he and Mahler drive us toward a closer consideration of the nature and importance of the self, which Winnicott describes as "the inherited potential which is experienced as a continuity of being." We have been calling this phenomenon the individual's story. Fairbairn's special interest is the nature and functioning of this self by focusing on self-esteem and self-concept development in the history of the individual.

But the salient theme running through the work of Mahler, Winnicott and Fairbairn concerns the very nature of the human developmental process. For these object relations theorists, the central dimension of psychological development is the movement from a state of complete dependence and a relative lack of differentiation between self and others to one of increasing independence and autonomy. For Fairbairn, it is more accurate to say a mature relationship is one which acknowledges interdependencies. Each of these theorists contributes important elements to our understanding of how attachments, separations and losses spur the maturation cycle.

The basic assumption of each of these then can be stated as follows: The struggle to preserve, correct or deepen relationships with important people throughout one's life begins in critical developmental periods in infancy. Moreover, this struggle continues throughout life with many of the same people. Styles are established and difficulties arise early and may last throughout life unless they are examined and modified in later relationships.

While looking at the contributions of Mahler, Winnicott and Fairbarin, the concept of developmental arrest, the role of transitional objects and the meaning of psychopathology will be examined. This will lead naturally to a discussion of the concept and meaning of the self, especially the issue of self-esteem. For it is the restoration of healthy self-esteem that is a prerequisite for psychological and spiritual healing. This topic will be taken up in the next chapter along with a discussion of its essentially pastoral dimension in a more complete way.

Separation and Individuation:
The Contribution of Margaret Mahler ▪▪

As was stated earlier on, it may have been Suttie who launched the notion of a primary, independent attachment instinct. Influenced by psychoanalysis, but not himself a psychoanalyst, Suttie claimed, as early as 1935, that a simple-attachment-to-mother constitutes a predominant instinctive repertoire in infants.[1] In his attack on Freud's theory of primary narcissism, he likened the attachment need to a need for company and said that it was operationally distinct from other physiological needs. Not until Margaret Mahler's work has there been empirical data supporting Suttie's claims.

Mahler, like Winnicott and Fairbairn, differs from Freud and other object relations theorists such as Jacobson and Hartmann in the way they conceptualize the main psychological significance of the role of objects (others) in the psychological growth of the infant. Mahler's position may be summed up as follows: the role of the object lies in its making self-integrity and independence possible, not in providing an occasion for instinctual investment and gratification.

In her work, Mahler pointed out that primary object needs and early forms of intrapsychic relations between mother and child are crucial for healthy development. She emphasized the personal aspect of relations, and stressed the issue of adaptation as a coming-to-terms with the world of other people. Pathological distortions of internal and external object relations have also been viewed by Spitz (1965), Winnicott (1965), Jacobson (1964), and Kohut (1977) as beginning with internal distortions originating in this mother/infant dyad. Premature ruptures or undue prolongation of the dual unity between infant and mother have important consequences for the way the child views the outside world. Again, optimal internalization of object relations, in tandem with phase appropriate opportunity for independent development, within a gradually expanding orbit of a facilitative mother-child relationship, is the core or heart of the maturation process. In other words, the development of internal structures for relationship and increasingly differentiated relations between self and others is essentially dependent upon a healthy attachment period.

In describing how this happens, Mahler's work has assumed the Freudian perspective but has departed in significant ways. She and her colleagues conclude that normal development proceeds from a stage of normal autism to a symbiotic period with four sequentially unfolding subphases in the separation–individuation process. The crucial element in this "unfolding" is always the mother-child interaction. Her assumption is that the child's chief struggle lies in reconciling and meeting the longing for independence and autonomy with an equally powerful urge to surrender and return to the original mother/infant fused state.

Mahler used Freud's bird-egg model to describe the infant as a closed system. This allowed her to discuss her ideas within the Freudian paradigm. The infant seems to be, at first, in a state of primitive hallucinatory disorientation in which need satisfaction seems to belong to this "unconditional omnipotent, autistic orbit" (cf Ferenczi).[2] This stage lasts through the first month of life. However, if we examine only the infant as the unit under investigation, we examine only half the dyad which consitutes the psychological being.

Stage two is the period of symbiosis. It is a stage of fusion between mother and infant and is characterized by the "delusion of a common boundary."[3] The first three months of life, from the point of view of the mother-infant dyad, are characterized by a give and take, clasping and letting go, by a basic rhythm of interaction. This initiates for the infant the experience of self and others, the "not me" and the "me." It also establishes the pattern of communication which is crucial for all interaction. The reciprocal nature of human interaction depends on an appreciation of this rhythm. In feeding, in play, in all activities involving another person, the infant begins, under normal circumstances, to appreciate this basic law of "give and take." (See Table 1, Developmental Timeline.)

Mahler then described the first subphase of this differentiation process in which the infant takes a first step away from the mother.[4] Within the symbiotic orbit, the two partners of the dyad

Table 1:

Margaret Mahler's *Developmental Timeline:*

A. *Weeks 1–2* Normal Autistic	B. *Weeks 3–4* Normal Symbiotic
Child: satisfaction of needs; Objectless state	*Child:* pre-objectal, unable to distinguish between self and other
Mother: total source of child's satisfactions	*Mother:* attends and reassures child

Weeks 5–8 Hatching	*Months 3–14* Practicing
Child: alert scanning, checking for mother's reactions	*Child:* crawling, climbing, interested in inanimate objects, uses mother as refueling station; with upright locomotive—psychological birth begins. (Love affair with the World—Greenacre, 1957)
Mother (or other): available, giving approval	*Mother:* relinquishes and allows for distances
	Father: encourages and consoles

C. *Months 15–18 and 18–24* Rapprochement	D. *Two to Three Years* Separation-Individuation

Child: separation anxiety, sometimes acute, experiences of failure complicate growth process, language ability means further ability to manipulate the environment, returns to parents but wants separateness. Between 18 and 24 months, child especially ambivalent; splits into good and bad

Child: beginning of consolidation of individuation and libidinal object constancy. Mahler's version: affectively charged, stable concept of self and others; child begins to believe in self and ability to stand on his own, despite pressure of others

Mother and Father: Seek to handle a new independence and new kinds of neediness; object constancy

Parents: See child as more and more independent, having personality of his own

may be regarded as polarizing the organizational structuring processes. The structures that derive from this double frame of reference represent a framework to which all experiences have to be related before they are clear and whole representations in the ego and the object world, as Jacobson stressed.[5] In this regard, Spitz called the mother "the auxiliary ego" of the infant in order to underline the important, life-giving function which she serves in a psychological sense and not just a physical sense.[6]

If normal autism then is a prerequisite for the development of the individuation process,[7] then normal symbiosis is the process in which the child invests in the mother, and within this vague dual unity forms the primal soil from which all subsequent human relationships grow.

Thus, Mahler and her group followed Spitz's notion of a pre-oedipal stage of bonding—the symbiotic phase—and believed that the vestiges of this stage "remain within us throughout the life cycle." The infant, and, later on, the adult, borrow confidence and power by feeling part of the omnipotent other. Helplessness is manageable because one feels merged with someone more powerful and able to provide.

The stage of separation-individuation lasts until the child is three. Its three subphases are hatching, practicing and rapprochement. In the earlier phases, the mother's chief task was to be responsive to the child's needs. Now, her task is to allow the child room to move away. She needs to encourage the toddler to let go and venture forth in the world. As the child acquires motor skills and masters the environment, the child depends on mother and other important people as anchors to reality, as "refueling stations" for the gaining of security, comfort and assurance that danger is not present.

The quality of these experiences helps determine the future ease or difficulty in relating to the environment as well as maintaining relationships with important care figures. Mahler and Gosliner hypothesized as early as 1955 that the images of love, for instance, as well as of the bodily and psychic self, emerge in ever-increasing memory traces of pleasurable (good) and unpleasurable (bad) instinctual, emotional experiences, and the prescriptions with which they become associated.[8] In other words, these early experiences of being allowed to venture forth in ease, of having been coddled and cared for, or the failure of important people to allow these things, has a direct relationship to the child's experience of others (outside world) and of oneself as good (worthy), or bad (unworthy) (internal world).

The drive toward individuation in the normal infant is an innate, powerful "given." Although this drive may be muted by protracted interference, it will be manifested in various ways along the separation-individuation process.[9] This is in sharp contrast to Freud who saw the regressive tendency in human development as gaining in ascendency. The principal condition for normal development and mental health, so far as pre-oedipal development is concerned, hinges on the attainment and continuing ability of the child to retain or restore self-esteem in a relatively constant manner, while at the same time meeting other needs.[10]

Mahler defines individuation as equivalent to the development of "intrapsychic autonomy," while separating deals with differentiating self from others, i.e., distancing and structuring boundaries between the self and the mother. If these processes have developed normally, the child becomes more and more a separate, distinct, autonomous person.

During the rapprochement subphase, the child returns to mother for continual comfort, after forays away from her, in order to make sure she is there and not upset with this separating and distancing. The mother is now more and more internalized. The child can trust that her love will continue despite these distances. Transitional objects—Mahler borrows here from Winnicott—help the child retain "mother" or a piece of mother in her physical absence. The child is thus able to retain an image of mother in her physical absence. This image of mother can be evoked when needed. "Object constancy" has developed so the child can assume the equilibrium—maintaining functions of mother within himself or herself, providing soothing and self-regulating narcissistic supplies to sustain self-esteem.

In addition, the child learns to tolerate ambivalence in relationships. As this capacity grows, the child no longer needs to relate to others as either good or bad, but can abandon defensive splitting of the objects in its environment and can accept others as composed of both good (pleasurable) and bad (unpleasurable) aspects.

This occurs near the end of the rapprochement subphase and is important for the development of another capacity within the child—the moral capacity. Accompanying the loss of omnipotence, the awareness of helplessness and the separateness of self, there naturally develops a concern with mother's displeasure, the potential loss of the love and concern of others who are important persons, now being carried "inside" the child. As the ego becomes structuralized, rules are internalized along with demands and ideals set forth by these important persons in the child's environment. The child's developing mastery of speech and ability to express a self in play, language, even art, help accomplish at least three things: they aid in (1) the maintenance of human contact, (2) the ability to scrutinize and evaluate the self, and (3) the mastery of important developmental tasks.

Developmental difficulties can occur during any of these phases. Symbiotic relatedness may continue when an anxious mother or overly eager mother tries to retain or push the child away. And some children may remain overly sensitive to the regulation of self-esteem by others in the environment. In narcissistic disorders, separation and a cohesive self have been achieved, but autonomy has not, and so others are needed to shore up self-esteem due to a growing and all-pervasive fear of an inability to survive outside of the symbiotic pattern. Making demands and refusing to accept limits becomes part of the relational style of such persons, especially when it comes to important care-takers.

Borderline disorders are characteristic of those who have not been able to rely on transitional objects as aids for separating or internalizing the mother. These individuals have not achieved a cohesive self and so are unable to differentiate a self from important others. This makes it almost impossible for them to differentiate themselves from their children. The loss of the object results in a dangerous threat to the regulation of self-esteem and threatens the very organization of the personality.

Both the borderline and the narcissistically wounded person attempts to maintain control over the environment (especially other persons) in order to extract what is needed to maintain a fragile self-esteem. When these persons have children of their own, such children become the pawns of their own psychopathology. Speaking of these two disorders in family therapy, Slipp has said, "Lacking internal tension-relieving mechanisms for sustaining narcissistic equilibrium in their psychic structures, they remain excessively sensitive to environmental self-objects to relieve tension and modulate self-esteem.[11]

More than anything else, Mahler's work has stressed the notion of developmental or adaptive style. During the subphase of rapprochement especially, the child learns to deal with separation anxiety. There are three subperiods consisting of, first, a beginning rapprochement period where the need for closeness held in abeyance during the toddler's practicing subphase (when exploration of environment had been all-consuming) is now re-enacted. The next subperiod consists of a rapprochement crisis when the child must handle intensely anxious feelings. The final subperiod consists of an individual's solution to the crisis with the emergence of the ability to carry the absent figure "inside." Basically, this period is a "coming to terms" with the mother and with being separate from her. The result is that the dilemma of being needful but separate, of wanting her present but not wanting her interference, of seeing mutual needs but experiencing different needs and feelings produces a pattern of true relating. The manner, style, confidence and trust with which this is done form fundmental personality characteristics which are consolidated in this period.

Mahler noted that as the rapprochement subphase progressed, children found more ways of coping with the mother's absence. For instance, they related to substitute adults and they engaged in symbolic play. They often invented forms of play that helped them to master the fact of the disappearance and reappearance of things, or their play tended to consist of social interaction, revealing early identifications with mother and father—as when playing a motherly figure or fatherly figure.

This crucial period of relating around physical absence has a great deal to do with success or failure of later attachments, separations and losses because it determines the relative ease or difficulty in handling anxiety in relationships. It helps determine the trust and care that go into forming, correcting and renegotiating difficult periods in "returning" to an important person.

Summarizing her own views of the critical clinical outcomes of this period, Mahler stressed that the success of this period determines the future development toward libidinal object constancy, i.e., the ability to form lasting relationships, the quality and quantity of later disappointments, the degree of castration anxiety and the fate of the oedipal complex and the development crises of adolescence.[12] All of this is dependent on a degree of object constancy and the internalization of parental demands, and so the kind of trust and the attitude toward the legitimate demands of others—a moral sense—which a child will develop are more than simply "colored by" these early critical periods. They emerge in them.

Mahler's work clarifies and dramatizes the important rhythm built into relationship processes—closeness and reliance are modulated with separation and distance. Her work also points to the importance that periods of physical absence serve in preparing the child for loss. The cyclic movement of attachment, separation and loss in infancy forge in the infant and child an identity which would otherwise not develop. The work of D.W. Winnicott sheds still further light on this dynamic process.

The Work of D.W. Winnicott: The Holding Environment ▪▪

Writing in a somewhat elusive style, Winnicott's theoretical essays have dealt with the even more elusive "emerging self." He rejected as unimportant Klein's death instinct and the role of envy and greed in children. Rather, he focused his attention on the "interaction" of the infant with its parents, a word he seems to prefer over such terms as "intrapsychic" (Klein) or "interpersonal" (Sullivan).

Winnicott has pointed out that the illusion of omnipotent control over mother, the result of an inability to distinguish self from non-self, creates in the child the trust and security needed to develop in order to "let go." Thus, Winnicott could speak of a "separation that is not a separation, but a form of union."[13] By this he meant that separation is a proces which is more a requisite for new forms of union between persons than a way of attaining a distance between persons.

It is the role of transitional objects to allow for the transference of dependent attachments toward healthy independence. As substitute mothers, those objects which the toddler selects (blanket, a stuffed animal, etc.) provide a warmth, comfort and constancy in mother's absence, allowing for forays away from her in order to test out the possibility of being on one's own. They are not internalized as are parental images, but remain "not me." When lost, they are not mourned. They serve a symbolic function as the root of fact and fantasy, helping inner and outer reality to become differentiated.

Winnicott believed that this tension between inner and outer reality is never really resolved. Rather the "mix" is a crucial aspect of the human capacity for creative living and interpersonal relationships. Objects in the outside world help build a created world which begins as an illusory inner reality. These objects help by relieving the strain between the subject's inner reality and the given in the environment. Art, religion and play are all creative activities combining these two realities—inner and outer. "Primary creativity and objective perception" are based on this important reality testing process.[14]

A second key developmental concept stressed by Winnicott is the importance of the failure of the mother to provide all that the child needs or wants. This failure to meet the child's every (unspoken) demand is important because without it an illusion of perfection and of omnipotence would prevail. This "bad mother" and "good mother" experience initiates the requirement to weigh, examine carefully, and ultimately to scrutinize the self in relationship to others.

The mother's role is also to provide a "holding environment" which is important for both the containment of the child's needs and the child's experience with separation. The mother's psychological holding of the child (good enough mothering) enables the child to move out, and from a distance to see the distinction between self and other, between inner and outer reality as well. This environment contains the child's aggressions without retaliation or abandonment, the two things the child fears most. Thus, further separation and individuation are possible.[15]

So, in the "good enough" holding environment, the infant sees that hatred does not necessarily destroy and that acceptance is possible. The infant experiences the self as constant and separate, and also experiences the object as separate and not completely controllable. Still, the child begins to realize that it does have an impact on the environment. After an "I am," Winnicott attests, the child needs to experience an "I am responsible." Consequences which are not overwhelming (within the holding environment) allow the child the opportunity to decipher the portion of individual responsibility which must be accepted. Thus, over the first few years of life—even before the Oedipus complex has risen—movement from narcissistic interests to concern for others develops naturally in the child. A "moral sense" develops from this caring, holding, helping environment. Its imperfection is in proper degree an asset, not necessarily or inevitably a debilitating condition. This would appear to be support for the claims made by Carol Gilligan on moral development, claims which will be examined in the next chapter.[16]

Winnicott observed that normal development will not occur if the mother is either too responsive and too accurate in all her responses. Nor will it occur if the mother and other care-takers are too distant. Intrusiveness and distance, and unavailability, are the chief problems. Unthinkable anxiety, Winnicott's phrase for the overwhelming experience of mother's absence or her excessive intrusiveness, is experienced as potential annihilation. Such a condition thwarts the development of an organizing agency. Like being abandoned, it is intolerable pain to the child.[17]

This lack of an organizing ego, insufficient ego development and integration, leads to the formation of what Winnicott called "a false self"—a compliant or imitative self "too fearful to exert itself." Developmental arrest, what Balint called "a basic fault," and Fairbairn and Guntrip call "a schizoid split," results in a fundamental inability to progress toward integration of good and bad mother introjects, and thus to accept the ambivalence of situations and the complexity of persons and oneself. This renders growth toward mature relationships impossible, since care and loving responses to mistakes and failures are not forthcoming.

Still, the quest for acceptance continues as the infant seeks a perfect, stable, all-accepting environment and is dissatisfied and angry when these are not forthcoming. "The mind has a root, perhaps its most important root, in the need of the individual, at the core of the self, for a perfect environment."[18] The yearning for wholeness is always present in this search for a caring environment.

In the important movement from total attachment to the sense of being separate, it is the mother's devotion, what Winnicott calls her "primary maternal preoccupation," that enables a self to feel sufficiently omnipotent, despite its nearly total need for sustenance from without. By mirroring the child back to the child, the mother begins teaching the child about the person who is the child, who is lovable, cute, worth noting and caring for. This more or less precise reflection of who and what the child is allows the child to appreciate distinctions between self and others. And, thus, it is the mother's resonance with the needs of the child which enables the child to begin to see its own needs.

The capacity to be alone then emerges, allowing the capacity to handle separations, the living with oneself. This capacity for being alone must develop gradually. If not, the child could be traumatized into a permanent split or schizoid condition. In such a condition it is as if the child decided deep within, "I will never reveal who and what I really am because it is not so lovable and that is why I was abandoned." How does this capacity to be alone develop? For this to occur, mother must be present in a non-demanding way, while allowing the child in her presence to manipulate the environment. Transitional objects allow for longer periods of physical separation until, finally, the infant discovers a life of its own.[19] All the while, the maturation of motor and language skills allows for ego autonomy in greater degrees. When these two processes are in synchronicity, then a minimal amount of anxiety is present.

The True and False Self ■■

The inability to meet and satisfy needs, as we have said, initiates anger, and a "false" separation process follows from it. The mother's anxiety over her failure or the child's failures can produce a "concern" (Klein would call this "guilt") over the pull or tug of the mother. The fear that the self is not capable, and the guilt of separation which mother may find intolerable, contribute to a split in the self. A "true self" and a "false self" develop over time and loses touch with the real needs. This true self is detached and atrophies when the failures of the child or the mother are gross. Its goal is to avoid expression and discovery at all costs. To be "discovered" would be equivalent to psychic death or annihilation.

Instead, a false self takes over, giving the impression of an existence fashioned out of and in accord with maternal expectations. This can take the form of grandiosity, or helplessness, whatever the perceived "needs" of the "other" are. The child then becomes the mother's image of who and what he or she ought to be. This false self functions to protect covertly the true self.[20]

Normally, the true self is nurtured in adequate, non-impinging, non-intrusive environments. The self becomes the "inherited potential which is experienced as a continuity of being." It acquires in its own way, at its own speed, a personal reality which takes account of the particular physical characteristics in which the psyche is embedded. It acknowledges all along its physicality.[21]

So even under ideal circumstances (and then such circumstances are no longer "ideal"), a tension exists between inner and outer reality, between subjective reality and objective reality. This core of creative tension is important because if unacknowledged, and undeveloped, developmental arrests and problems in the environment become more difficult to overcome. Weakened self-esteem, and inexperience with success from creative manipulation of both inner and outer reality, in attempts to change and to bring that reality (inner or outer) into conformity with one another, debilitate the growth process. On a more positive note we can say that the seeds of the creative self are given in the imperfection of the world and the people in it who are the child's caretakers.[22]

Winnicott also helps us to see that the infant's psychic vulnerability is the bedrock for a core vulnerability—that "sacred, uncommunicated, most worthy of preservation" aspect of the child's psyche. Fear of exploitation creates this impenetrable core in even the most firmly anchored and loved individuals. In healthy self-development, the self is isolated but not insulated, he reminds us in *Maturation Process and the Facilitating Environment.*[23] This sets up a tension necessary for mature dependence and healthy independence in relationships throughout life. There must be an openness but not excessive openness. Extremes such as total vulnerability and elusiveness must be avoided. A directness in relationship must seek to outweigh cryptic ambiguity. In addition, loyalty and consistency must be weighed against destruction and rearrangements in relationships.

Winnicott's emphasis on balances between inner and outer reality, between openness and caution in relationships, etc., presumes the development of complex ego structures, which in turn presumes an oversight function, a self. We now turn to Fairbairn for a more detailed and a fuller explanation of the role and process of both ego and self development.

W.R.D. Fairbairn: Coping with Ambiguity ▪▪

We have already noted that the underlying principle upon which Fairbairn based his work was that the libido is not as much pleasure-seeking, but object-seeking.[24] Like Sullivan, Fairbairn concentrated the whole of his method and research on the study of relationships. Unlike Sullivan, however, he stressed the problem of internalized objects as the source of psychic health or illness. In this way he is closer to Klein.

From this basic proposition of the built-in drive to seek relationship with others, Fairbairn interpreted stages of development as "techniques" employed by the ego for regulating commerce with others in the outside world. The ego, then, is a structure with its own dynamic aims. Intrapsychic conflict is not to be interpreted, as did Freud, in terms of an id-ego model, but more in the terms of a split in the states of the ego, that is, in the ego itself. As can be seen in Kohut's work, this lends itself to a more sophisticated conception of the development of the self and accounts more fully for deep-seated problems which develop prior to the oedipus complex. Fairbairn, then, posits no id, but rather ego structures with their own aims and impulses. How, then, does he explain psychic organization?

Early states of infantile dependence cause an ego to emerge from an autistic state, accomplished primarily by identification with the object. The ego then matures to states of dependence based on differentiation of the self from the object. Complete independence is impossible in the sense that the self cannot exist outside relationships with other significant human beings. Such a state would be psychotic.

Like Mahler, psychological development for Fairbairn takes the form of stages of separation and individuation, and, like Kohut, development occurs as the self differentiates from the object: one knows a self as opposed to, in relation to, and apart from others. Three stages are important in this process, which occurs on the level of both ego and self: infantile dependence leads to a transitional stage and finally to adult dependence.

Underlying all this is a basic schizoid split in the ego which develops as the child realizes that the care of others cannot always be counted on. To love or not to love, to be attached or not to be attached is the infant's (and the adult's) dilemma. This is further complicated as the frustrations of the child lead to a desire to destroy the object that is needed for survival, both physically and psychically. This is the real cause of a split in the ego. How does this split come about and how does it function?

Fairbairn explains that the child cannot help but experience the mother as both good and bad. The bad mother is threatening, in fact too threatening to leave in outer reality, like some monster which cannot be controlled and so can too easily scare. Thus, the child's internalized object is experienced as both exciting and rejecting. Here Fairbairn distinguishes between several "egos" at work. A central ego, fearing both the exciting and the rejecting mother, further represses this split object. The internalized, repressed object is actually three different objects: a good mother, an exciting mother, and a rejecting mother.

That ego of the child interested in the repressed objects is also repressed and thus split off from the rest of the ego. In other words, the "me" I cannot allow myself to see directly and admit to is an anxious and needy infant wanting the mother and wanting to control all of her. This split-off ego is called the libidinal ego (the ego attached to the exciting objects). And the ego attached to the rejecting object, called the internal saboteur, is the anti-libidinal ego. Thus, the first and best defense against objects which cannot be controlled by the infant—and this remains true for life—is to internalize it.

But good objects are internalized as well. Unfortunately, Fairbairn does seem to concentrate on the internalization of bad objects. However, Guntrip clarifies this issue by stressing that good objects are internalized as memories and so build up the positive side of the psychic structure. An analogy exists in the way that food is taken in and digested. Good, nutritious food is metabolized, becoming part of the body's source of energy. That part of the food which is not nutritious or good remains foreign and retains its identity as a foreign substance until eliminated.

Traditionally, this internalization process is known as "introjection." It includes the central idea of taking in and making a part of oneself some set of representations, traits, evaluations, and prohibitions of others. Incorporation and identification do not completely express Fairbairn's ideas. He stresses in this concept of internalization the fact that some parts of that which is introjected remain foreign and continue to remain so. What he has done is give us a way of conceptualizing the experience of having a split will, an unintegrated part, or "pieces" deep within, which cannot be fully accepted, that are not really "me." Normally, identification and introjection are not discussed this way. As Eagle has indicated, "the hallmark of identification, a process in which what is taken in is more fully assimilated and integrated, is a characteristic feel of intentionality, will, activity."[25] Fairbairn wants to retain the element of the unintegrated, unassimilated, "objective" other which is within us, the part of us we cannot "own."[26]

Motivation ■■

Fairbairn's theory of motivation is explained in his work, *Object Relations Theory of Personality.*[27] By stressing that an impulse is inseparable from its structure, Fairbairn believed that the fundamental dynamic of drive and motivation was more compatible with modern physics and thus restored the personal will, thought by Freud to be impersonal. Impulses were conceived of as "packets of energy distinct and separate from ego," the agency which, along with the superego, uses energy for various physical and psychical activities.[28]

In traditional Freudian theory, the id is structureless, energy is directionless and the ego is all process, without its own energy source. This nineteenth century model from the physics of the day separates structure from function, energy from mass. For Fairbairn, this anachronistic notion distorts by separating out instead of seeing the intrinsic mix of the two—energy and object. The result is to superimpose upon the psychic process an artificial distinction between activity and energy presumed to be "feeling" the activity. To Fairbairn, ego structures are themselves energy.[29]

The consequences of this model are important. For, instead of focusing on the utility of others, the thrust of the organism is already and innately *toward* others regardless of their ability to satisfy or remove frustration. Thus, the human infant is adaptive and creative of relationships, and this adaptivity and creativity is built up into the biological survival structure of the human organism. Moreover, erogenous zones of the body provide the "occasions" for contact and are thus modes of relatedness with others.

Within this structural model, a model of innate relatedness, aspects of relationships can be assessed in a different light. Aggression, for example, can be handled theoretically as something which arises not spontaneously, but as a reaction to frustration of primary motivational aim, i.e., contact with others. It is neither a component of nor transformation of libido, but has its own distinct energy. It is not a natural, automatic drive, but a secondary, derivative one.

Pathology can be redefined as well. In the older framework, pathology was seen as the result of conflicts over pleasure-seeking impulses. Within Fairbairn's framework, pathologies are reflective of disturbances and interferences in relationships with others-who-matter. The therapeutic process, moreover, does not consist in resolving unconscious conflicts over how to achieve satisfactions, but is rather concerned with another. The crucial aspect for healthy maturation is the capacity for rich, intimate, mutuality with another human being. Pleasure-seeking, in its pure and simple form, is reflective of a deterioration of the natural (object-related) libidinal functioning.[30]

This can be put another way. The fundamental conflict in pathology is between mature independence and dependencies, and a regression or reluctance to abandon infantile ties to undifferentiated objects. The underlying fear in all this is the fear of the loss of contact. Thus, the maturation process is, at heart, the development of the capacity for accepting separation and differentiation and so accepting the kinds of losses which are inevitable in relationships.

Fairbairn's Developmental Theory ■■

Like Klein, then, Fairbairn believed that "positions" better characterize developmental levels and not psychosexual stages. Bodily zones become the focus for maturational hurdles or the vehicles for difficulties to be negotiated in relationship with important caretakers. The infant's helplessness forces a fusion with one better able to function in order to survive in a hostile world. Through the process of primary identification the infant "cathects an object not yet differentiated from the cathecting subject."[31] The crucial factor in all this is the infant's lack of differentiation.[32]

Through experiences of the inability of the care-takers to meet the needs for satisfaction, and through the growing capacity for self-help, for manipulation of the environment, and the use of language, the infant experiences pleasure at being its own source of survival (inflation). Through failure and the recognition of re-alistic limits of independence, the child, in increasingly wider cir-cles of social contact, learns to rely on others as well as itself when its own capacities are not adequate to meet the demands of the world.[33] This lesson remains true throughout life.

The transitional phase, first seen dramatically in childhood, marks the difference between dependence and mutuality. It means renunciation of compulsive attachments to objects of pri-mary identification and merger. Second, it is a movement in favor of a relationship based on differences and exchanges. The child learns to accept the different capacities, styles, and types of ex-change of which significant persons are capable. Third, and most important, the child in the transitional process experiences a self as separate, loved, welcomed and valued for its attachment, loy-alty and dependability as well as for its uniqueness, difference, and separateness. In the process, infantile internal objects, split in order to be controlled, are resolved and overcome. This re-stores the original integrity and richness of the ego. We are healed by the acceptance and respect of others. What then happens when relationships are unsatisfying or unhealthy?

Unsatisfying, external relations produce in the ego the urge to create a compensatory internal object. The splitting of the ego is the consequence of the proliferation of internal objects since different portions of the ego remain related to different internal objects. This is the source of the original fragmentation of the ego and the need for its resolution and healing. It is the result of want-ing to remain dependent or of being unable to separate for some reason or other.[34] Unhealthy development and pathology is pro-duced by a clash of wills, by selfishness and self-centeredness in human relationships. In traditional religious language, this has been called sin.

Conclusions ▪▪

It seems clear that the child within the family unit is a com-plex and rich phenomenon. The study of these psychic and social processes, however, may give the impression of an excessively clinical examination. Some object relations theorists do seem to fall into error in this way. For example, Otto Kernberg has summarized a great deal of object relations theory in an attempt to comprehend the phenomenon of borderline psychoses. His book, *The Borderline Condition and Pathological Narcissisms*,[35] has identified specific phases of developmental arrest during childhood that result in deficiencies of identity and pathology using self-object phenomenology. He has outlined the five tasks of childhood as follows: (1) self-object differentiation—I am not you and you are not me; (2) internalization of the good and bad mother—as a prerequisite for approaching complexity and ambiguity in relationships; (3) integration of ambiguites—coming to terms with the mixture of good and bad in others; (4) development of object constancy—ability to carry others within us and so endure absence, separation and even loss; (5) structuralization of the psyche.

What he and many others fail to note is that these occur within a cycle of continuous attachments, separations and losses. It is the experience of surviving self, of coming out of a relationship stronger, that accounts for the growth of self-esteem. It is also the coming to awareness of the meaning of others, reflections on who and what is real value, that gives birth to the self as the chief actor and creator in a story that is unique. This historical narrative element is missing in many of these theorists. Without drawing attention to this quality which the psyche possesses Fairbairn, Kernberg and others run the risk of over-simplifying or run the risk of "reifying" human psychic processes. This leads us to a more complete discussion of the self in its complexity which we take up in the next chapter.

In order to share one's story—even if only to attempt to clarify its elements—a sense of the self and its worth must exist. Some experience of self as actor and creator of a story is the necessary foundation for the relational process. It is as well the necessary prerequisite for the healing which occurs in effective therapy.

▪ 5 ▪

THE DEVELOPMENT OF SELF-ESTEEM:
Object Relations Theory and
the Role of Therapy

Introduction ▪▪

▪ The capacity to form attachments and the capacity to love oneself are directly related. They are mutually supportive capacities. From a psychodynamic perspective, the child's narcissistic love is the necessary precursor of object love and the foundation for valuing a self. For, as the self emerges, it does so in key attachments—we know ourselves in relation to others—and, more importantly, we sharpen our understanding, develop and grow in our self-concept as we experience separation from those who are our first caretakers. This, as we have seen in the previous chapter, is at the heart of the separation and individuation process. Ultimately, however, we have a significant experience of the self in the survival of losses. Without separation and loss, the child would not experience the self as surviving. Its worst fears—of annihilation and abandonment—could not be mastered if the child could not survive the loss of the old relationships and so form new relationships from those which have ended in some way.

This chapter will concern itself with the manner in which the self grows and matures in the developmental process and in the therapeutic. After examining the concept of self in object relations terms, criticisms of object relations theory with regard to self-concept development will be discussed. This leads directly to a definition of pathology and a discussion of the role of therapy as a healing of the self.

Child developmentalist, Jerome Kagan, in "The Emergence of

Self,"[1] writes that a self can be said to emerge around the second year of life. A set of abilities indicating a "sense of self" becomes apparent as five different "competencies" mature. These are: recognition of the past, retrieval of prior schemata, inference, awareness of one's potentiality for action, and awareness of self as an entity with symbolic attributes.[2] The degrees of connectedness among these are admittedly obscure, but the first four are presumed to be due to an incipient awareness of the self. These are described as necessary "but not sufficient attributes" or competencies. Moreover, the foundation for both moral evaluation of aggression and for self-consciousness are universal milestones of the second year of life. Increasingly, child developmentalists stress the important and crucial nature of early experiences as they affect and impact an entity of the personality which is deeper and more fundamental than ego and superego, or the id-ego-superego apparatus. What exactly is this "self" about which Kagan and others speak?

Definition of Self in Object Relations Terms ■■

The variety of good and bad self-object experiences throughout the duration of the separation-individuation process establishes and develops an inner organization of wholeness, cohesion, continuity (history), goals and values. This inner organization is the self. According to Mack, the psychological development of humans depends on the development of the self, not over and against others; rather we are speaking of a self-in-relation to others.[3] The more mature a relationship, according to Fairbairn, the more it involves two distinct selves and the less it is characterized by "primary identification," that is, the internalized other. The uniqueness of this relatedness is such that it is its own reality, an independent entity. Psychology, however, at this time can only assert the necessity of seeing the self as a system whose boundaries do not coincide with the boundaries either of the body or of what is properly called consciousness.[4]

This state of primary identification is really a failure to differentiate between the self and the object; it is a failure in separation-individuation. When and to the extent that such a state persists, a compulsory quality toward the object colors the relationship. This is the schizoid problem according to Fairbairn. It belongs to the pre-moral level of self-development and psychic life. The depressive problem on the other hand exists on the level of psychic life and belongs to the pathological moral level. Since each person has within the self a "split" due to inadequate, less-than-perfect care, a "wound," if you will, must be healed in relationship. Pathology then represents the extreme wound to the self. It occurs when those care-takers who are given to the child, or individual, are incapable of helping heal the wounded self, due perhaps to their own wounded and unavailable selves.

Basch emphasizes the "symbolic" aspect of this entity we call the self. He defines the self as "the uniqueness that separates experiences of one person from those of all others while conferring a sense of cohesion and continuity on disparate experiences of the individual throughout his or her life. "The self is the symbolic transformation of experience into an overall goal-oriented construct."[5] Having a hierarchy of goals is indicative of a deeper, more fundamental belief in the self as worthwhile. Valuing the self, then, is necessary for the continuation of the symbolic function. Self-esteem, or self-valuation, states Huizenga, results when narcissistic self-love is transformed into autonomous ego functions by means of which we value our accomplishments and regulate our well-being.[6]

Kohut, however, focuses his definition on the bi-polar nature of the self and its development. Prior to the separation of self-objects, i.e., those others who are so psychologically fused that we must speak of them as symbiotically related, there is little opportunity to speak of a self in any accurate way. However, when the self-objects are internalized and subsequent experiences of self-other differences forces an evaluation of the self-objects, then a self is being born. In separation-individuation terms, we are referring to the movement from a reliance on self-objects for self-definition and self-esteem, to self-cohesion fueled by the child's own inner ambitions, values and ideals.

The child who is welcomed and mirrored lays down the rudiments of ambitions at one pole which is imbued with grandiosity and perfection. Permitted to merge with the idealized perfection and power of those who minister to emerging needs, the child acquires the rudiments of ideals and goals at a second pole. It is the relationship between poles, the strength and harmony of their interaction, and the skills and talents which are elaborated through nature and nurture which define the cohesive nuclear self, the continuous self in time and space.[7]

As Cohen *et al.* have stressed, it is "the capacity to fantasize for their child a limitless potential while performing a mirroring, affirming, and controlling function which is the foundation and hallmark of mature narcissism, of then mature and responsible parenthood."[8]

Thus, throughout the developmental cycle, experiences of an other's response are intrinsic to the creation of necessary structures for considering the "value" of one's action. Actions of another, responses, especially emotional responses, more than anything else signal to the child that his or her differences must be noted internally for defense and protection against misunderstanding and rejection. Which reactions and whose ought to be noted? To Kohut, narcissistic libido (self-love) is a form of psychic energy that supports the cohesion and continuity of the self, by maintaining equilibrium when devaluation and rejection are forthcoming.[9]

The Development of Self-Esteem   ■■

In their overview to a collection of essays on the development and sustaining of self-esteem in childhood, editors Mack and Ablon state: "In each state of development after infancy the achievement of a sense of positive self-worth contributes not only to the child's sense of well-being but also to the quelling of his fears for his actual survival."[10] The fundamental need to experience one's existence as valued comes at first from without, from others, but must, for protection and for important developmental purposes, be internalized as soon as possible.

The protection of self-esteem is a central task of childhood. The denial of wrongdoing and blaming inanimate objects for mistakes or accidents are but two examples of the many manifestations of this "first" task. In other words, the development of the self-esteem, to recall Sullivan's use of the term, minimizes anxiety and, if it does not develop early, inhibits the child from progressing psychologically or cognitively, or perhaps physically as well.

For Sullivan, self-esteem is that vast organization of experiences concerned with protecting the self.[11] Trials and difficulties, then, are the chief source of devastating emotional events which constitute blows to self-esteem, forcing the "setting into place" of a system for its regulation and maintenance. The trials of separation and loss (from important care-takers) are perhaps the "chief" difficulties to master.

Each phase of development, according to Cotten, has its special requirements. She noted three main sources of self-esteem: the esteem of others, competence in carrying out tasks, and the self viewed as a selective filter of these first two functions of sources.[12] Pathology results from a failure of one of these sources, or "strands."

In infancy, it is the esteem of others which creates a positive emotional environment so that self-love can develop. This self-love provides specific information about what is worthwhile and lovable about the child to the child. Eventually, the opinions and feelings of others become a part of the intrapsychic structure of the self[13] (Fairbairn's "primary identification").

Later on, the mastery of skills and achievements is the "basis in reality" for a self-esteem which takes the environment seriously. Just as approval and love from accepting parents leads to pleasure and pride in "being" someone, the real successes a child has had will foster his or her pleasure in "doing." In other words, healthy self-esteem regulation depends increasingly on a competent child developing within a supportive and praising world of adults. And, with the development of cognitive abilities (Piaget) and a growing sense of trust in the world through autonomous behavior (Erikson), the "self" acts more and more as a filter regulating the way various sources—internal and external—affect self-esteem. The self interprets the meaning of events—makes inferences, to use Kagan's word—and notes opinions of others which are not one's own.

The nature and types of self-perceptions are interesting to note. The first self-perceptions accrue from bodily pleasure and pain. These sensorimotor perceptions are the first "filter" and lay the foundation for bodily self-awareness and the body-self schema. This body-self schema serves as an important source of self-perception throughout the life cycle. Psychosexual development (Freud) contributes to the early body-self schemata through differentiation and the channeling of drives.

In the toddler phase, both praise and acceptance are balanced by the equally important role of limit-setting and guidelines. Coopersmith has identified parental acceptance and limit-setting as two major conditions which are present in the lives of children with high self-esteem. The battling of wills is an important aspect of the creation of self-esteem because of the child's need to recognize the interrelations into which he or she has been born, i.e., the consequences of actions and the effect these have on others.[14] In this, the child learns the legitimate needs of others and thus learns of his or her own legitimate needs.

As Mahler *et al.* and Kagan have noted, the child in the second year of life begins to refer to itself as "I," attesting to the formation of this self-concept.[15] In moving away from significant others, the child's self emerges more clearly. Reapproaching these significant persons (as in the rapprochement subphase) helps integrate separations and attachments and is thus a crucial period in the formation of the self. Without this integration, complete detachment (autism) or complete dependency would develop. For the self experiences itself most completely in returning to "objects" which were successfully left behind. This Mahler calls the "fulcrum" of psychological development. It is a "milestone in self-esteem regulation" if the child can successfully move from periods of self-preoccupation (at first it is the self as center of the universe) to seeing self as a part of a network of competent, powerful people.

The third phase of self-esteem maintenance and regulation occurs when the radius of people affecting the child's life is significantly broadened. A firm foundation must be established prior to this period and concomitantly a growing range of competencies must develop.[16] By this period, we can begin to differentiate the child's self-concept. That is, as Rosenberg has described self-concept, it is made up of the child's self-picture: what he or she would like to be, what others want him or her to be, and what he or she actually is. Thus, Rosenberg refers to an extant self, a desired self and a presenting self. Children gain a broader, richer picture of themselves, as well as a more accurate one, as they expand the repertoire of activities and the number of significant persons to whom they are attached.[17] The self, then, organizes itself into a hierarchy of what is important, according to "the principle of psychological centrality." That is, beliefs, attitudes and values are given different weight, positive and negative, depending on the importance and relevance they have for the self's survival.[18]

Self-esteem regulation, then, is vulnerable to a host of situations, especially those of an interpersonal nature. Realistic and attainable goals in this period and interpersonal encounters are crucial ingredients. Excessive dependency needs, anxious separations, and traumatic losses tend to increase the child's vulnerability. Unless these are satisfactorily negotiated, the child becomes "stuck" in the cycle and suffers a blow to self-esteem, rendering other positive self-esteem factors impotent to shore up the wounded self.

The next phase is that of the school-age child where the three sources of self-esteem information are integrated and the self is able to serve as the filter for that which comes from important others and from the environment. Traumatic events such as divorces, overly stressed or anxious parents, new environments (e.g., new school) and the losses which flow from these separations can loosen the fragile self-esteem of the child whose ability to regulate self-esteem is already undeveloped or weakened. Information from others, believed to be valued by parents and society, and from the mastery of skills believed to be necessary for a self-definition (e.g., doing what peers can do), has increasing impact even as parents continue to affect the child's self-esteem rather directly. The absence of praise from parents, then, no matter how competent the child or accepting other adults are, can damage self-esteem and wound the self.

Adolesence, the final phase in an examination of self-esteem regulations in childhood, is characterized by a re-evaluation, and a refocusing of all that went before. A new consolidation of self-esteem is worked for by the emerging adolescent as he or she tests out the skills and self-definitions built up in childhood. Uncertain of the accuracy of the opinions of important caretakers, the adolescent seeks to redefine his or her identity and self-conception based more and more on the evaluation of the outside world and those relationships characterized by a new intimacy, now biologically possible and important.

Mature self-esteem regulation, then, occurs when a person

can sustain a relatively high level of self-esteem by means of the realistic valuing of skills and accomplishments and can rely on internal standards of achievement and moral virtue that are flexible and appropriate to the person's life situation. This results in the capacity to be appropriately concerned with approval of valued others and groups.

It is important to note that shift from reliance on external sources to internal structures is never completely accomplished. This is perhaps the chief aspect of psychological dependency which necessitates that we view total independence as immature. For, completely ignoring the opinions of others and of traditions where value and beliefs are treasured, may be a pathological retreat into the self. It may mark the presence of a narcissistic wound to the self, as both Miller and Kohut have noted.[19]

Criticisms of the Object Relations View of Self-Development ■ ■

Several important criticisms have been put forward which impact this description of the development and sustaining of self-esteem. They come from within the psychodynamic school of thought as well as from others. Before we are in a position to discuss childhood pathology and the process of therapy as a healing of the self in relationship, we need to take note of the contributions of several child development psychologists concerned with self-definition. Chodorow, for example, has criticized the tendency within psychoanalysis and in object relations theory to ignore important differences of cognitive development. She has contributed to our understanding of the child's perception of a self-in-relationship from a cognitive perspective. First, this has important ramifications for intrapsychic development and, second, it broadens our understanding of interpsychic life.

In her book, *The Reproduction of Mothering*, Chodorow depicts motherhood as a biological necessity restricted to one gender while parenting is the responsibility of both genders (with ramifications for self-definition).[20] In the developmental process as a whole, a complete self is transmitted by both parents. If only one gender is involved in the transmission, then an incomplete representation of the whole self is passed on to the child. A healthy self, then, is derived from both parents for healthy development of a self-means development of the bisexual nature of the child. The domination of the lives of children by one gender produces self-perceptions and self-descriptions which are faulty, i.e., skewed to one pole.

Chodorow notes that object relations between girls and their mothers are necessarily different from those of boys and their mothers. She cites Deutsch[21] to show that for girls, from the very onset of life, the choice of a heterosexual object is rendered extremely difficult because her first object choice is a woman and so she must transfer her first object choice from a female to a male in order to mature in her self-definition as a woman. To Chodorow, a girl's relationship with her father is a reaction to, interwoven with, a competition for primacy with her relationship with her mother. This renders her sexual development a more difficult developmental task. Retaining her intense tie to her mother (involved are such issues as primary identification, primary love, dependency and separation), she must build her oedipal attachments later on to both mother and father.

In theory, she writes, a boy resolves his oedipal complex by repressing his attachment to his mother. He is, therefore, ready in adulthood to find a primary relationship with someone like his mother. In this a boy recapitulates an intense exclusive relationship: first an "identity," then a dual unity, and finally a two-person relationship emerges.

A girl, however, retains an "internalized early relationship, including its implications for the nature of her definitions of self, and internalizes these other relationships in addition to and not as replacements for it."[22] The result is no absolute change of objects choice, and thus no exclusive attachment to the father. Still, a father's behavior, his availability and his role are crucial for the development of mature heterosexuality. Usually, since most fathers are less present than are mothers, girls retain an involvement with their mothers and oscillate emotionally between her and the males in their lives. Because women continue to experience heterosexual relationships in a triangular context, men never become exclusive objects of affection, according to Chodorow. The important point here is the way gender influences self-definition through the likely object choices which are present in the first years of life. Mahler, Winnicott, Fairbairn and Klein ignore this crucial element.

Carol Gilligan's concern is also with the impact of gender on self-definition.[23] She builds her argument from a different source, and is not specifically concerned with the limitations in object relations theory. She studied the self-definitions of boys and girls in an attempt to determine whether these would significantly impact their moral development. Her conclusion is that girls see the world as composed of webs of relationships, whereas boys see it in hierarchical fashion. Girls understand the world as cohering through human connectedness rather than through systems of rules, which is a distinctly made preference. Thus, in a world of relationships, the awareness of connections between people gives rise to a recognition of responsibility for one another, and the perception of a need for response.

This perception of a self-in-relationship leads naturally to the development of an ethic of care, whereas the hierarchical perspective leads to an ethic of justice. These further impact the self-understanding of children as they mature. The tendency of theorists to see the patterns of growth and development as revolving around continuous states of separation and the making of distinctions leads to an equation of development with separation. It results in a failure to represent the reality of connection both in love and in work. The lives of women and their own self-understanding reveal an "imbeddedness" in lives of relationship, an orientation to interdependence and a subordination of achievement to care.

This hypothesis supports the central thrust of our thesis here, and it raises important considerations about the way gender affects self-definition. Boys may be more concerned with independence and competence than are girls, but to what extent are they expected to do so? The nature of their ties to mother and then to others may seriously differ from those girls, and, if so, what are the implications of their cyclic struggles with attachment, separation and loss of the object?

Chodorow raises the issue of differing developmental processes on the intrapsychic level in infancy and childhood. As the girl becomes more conscious of her gender—beginning in the second year of life—she will take different cues from her relationship with her mother than will a boy who perceives his relationship with her differently. As we have noted, how the pre-oedipal developmental process differs for boys and girls is not handled in Mahler, Winnicott or Fairbairn and remains a weak aspect of object relations theory. Furthermore, the therapeutic process may differ depending on the gender of the therapist. Still, the opportunity to successfully complete the cycle of attachment, separation and loss, leading to rebirth and healing (or renewal), is at the heart of the therapeutic process and may transcend gender considerations.

Therapy and the Healing of the Self ▪▪

As we have seen in the previous chapters, Mahler and Winnicott, Fairbairn, Sullivan and Klein have contributed to our understanding of the way a self develops and matures in relationships. Martin Buber wrote, "Mutual confirmation is essential to becoming a self—a person who realizes uniqueness precisely through relations with other selves."[24] How then ought we to understand the process of healing in therapy? What constitutes the nature of the therapeutic process such that healing takes place?

We have noted the development of a hierarchy of valued persons who have an impact on self-esteem. This is the result of the selectivity factor or "filtering" which occurs for self-esteem regulation. The child must determine who will be allowed to influence the development and sustaining of self-esteem. This is an important survival skill or task. Praise and respect from others does not necessarily enhance self-esteem since the child must value the person giving it as a potential source of information about his or her worth.[25]

For Fairbairn, ambition, value and ideals are built up with self-esteem goals taking precedence and determining their position in the hierarchy of values. Values, for Fairbairn, are the child's expression of universal object relations needs. Just as in the symbiotic phase when the mother supports the child's narcissim by giving comfort, appropriate stimulation and protection, during the course of therapy, the child, after a time of testing, values the support and comfort of the therapist within the holding environment. Just as this experience and those within the rapprochement phase of separation-individuation are the precursors of a sense of cohesion and continuity, necessary for healthy self-esteem regulation, the therapeutic relationship must over time become a foundation for re-examination and reintegration of a sense of self so that a new cohesion may emerge. This is the essence of the healing process. If mutual confirmation is essential to becoming a self, it is also necessary in the healing of a wounded self.

Object relations theorists help us to appreciate several other elements of the therapeutic process as well. Since the therapist is dealing with a child whose self-definition has suffered in the trouble and trauma that has preceded therapy, it will be important for him or her to create an environment where care and approval can be experienced. The same holds true for work with the parents whose own self-esteem has been wounded.

The child's growing capacity to be alone during the sessions is a sign of the child's self-cohesion and growing health. By helping the child to master the world and to understand the problems of parental figures, as well as understand his or her own feelings, the therapeutic process aids the integration of ego accomplishments, ego supports and self-understanding. Thus, the child can internalize the support coming from the therapist, just as in normal development the child internalizes the support of parents. The child, when alone, without the therapist, can retain the therapist's warmth, approval and acceptance. In this the child experiences himself or herself as important and valued and can thus value a self.

The healing process, then, is one which begins by securing a firm attachment. In this, a value is placed on the relationship by the child, something crucial for healing the wounded self. Once in place, the child can experiment with ideas and feelings, and can discuss confusing and complex matters which he or she does not comprehend. Mastery is built over internal as well as external worlds. The self as a filter of opinions and feelings of others can screen out harmful and disruptive or negative information about the self. This occurs because the therapist mirrors the child back to the child—thus its valuable qualities, its very self, can be once again valued, and, as Kohut has emphasized, made firm. "Mutuality" involves patterns of re-engagement, renewing and deepening of the modes of communication and relatedness. These patterns shift, of course, for they are linked to the internal states of both the child and, in this case, the therapist. In sum, the therapeutic process heals through the care-giving (attachment), communication, joint problem-solving, and separations which enable "mutuality" to develop.

Therapist as Parental Figure or as Transitional Object ▪▪

Kahn and Banks in their book on the sibling bond have noted that both Winnicott and Mahler see siblings as important transitional figures or objects when parents are incapable or unavailable, or when they pull away from the child in normal healthy development.[26] Sensitivity and a willingness to subordinate one's own needs seem to be the only two requirements for a person to serve as a transitional object.[27] This recognition of the ability of others to be transitional objects has important consequences.

During key phases of therapy the therapist is immersed in a relationship with the child which is in one way "a primary one," and thus recapitulates the parental dynamic of attachment, separation and loss, especially at the conclusion of the therapy, or the therapist may be seen to provide the child with a transitional figure. In some situations, depending on the type and severity of the problem as well as on the stage of the therapeutic process, the therapist plays one role, then another. These roles may last for a good amount of time. Like a parent, the therapist may be fostering mastery over anxiety and tolerance for certain levels of it, and may be helping in the expression of needs and feelings. As a transitional object for the child, the therapist may be providing empathy and support and acceptance which allows the child the ability to tolerate feelings and confusions.

Summary: Contributions to Theory and Therapy ▪▪

Both Sullivan and Fairbairn have stated that the child shapes structures or distorts his own experiences, behavior and self-perceptions to maintain the best possible relatedness with the parental figure. Critics of Mahler have stated that there is evidence to suggest that this active capacity is present from the very beginning, and that so-called "normal autism" is a fiction. The infant, such critics propose, is never in a state of complete objectlessness, complete non-differentiation between self and other. Therefore, normal autism is not an accurate term for the earliest phase of development.[28] These critics believe that the infant from the very earliest has the capacity and ability to form a rudimentary conception of itself and others and to differentiate between the two.[29] Psychological and biological birth are then simultaneous. From the start, non-genuine, inadequate relationships between the child and its care-taker(s) produce a split (Fairbairn's "schizoid state") in order to protect itself. The fear and anxiety which come from inadequate care need to be healed in all children.

Psychopathology may have its roots in the relationships which children are given and begin to develop from the earliest. The personality of the child can only shape itself in complementarity to that of its parents. In normal development, those areas of the child which are complemented by non-anxious and emotionally available parents are developed and expanded in normal ways. Those which have a disruptive impact on development are those which are "disturbed." That is, these areas of the child's personality are undeveloped and not available for use in dealings with the world.

To Fairbairn, psychology is the study of relationships of the individual to its objects, and psychopathology is the study of the relationships of the ego to its individual objects. Fairbairn calls attention to the internal residue of early interactions within key relationships and Sullivan accents operational concepts which emphasize the tendency to avoid anxiety, based on anticipation of past experiences. Together, these two approaches highlight the importance of the way key attachments, separations and losses have been negotiated and the impact that the process has had on internal "blocking," as well as anxiety in anticipation of new trauma. Again, the result is a wounded self that develops from such poverty of experience or from faulty experience. The self has not experienced "itself" as surviving intact—and healthier—so it believes that attachments, separations or losses are unnegotiable, dangerous, and potentially annihilating. Again, since problems in dealing adequately with the environment and distortions in relationship represent a blow to the self, the therapeutic process must at some level be a healing of the self.

Conclusion ▪▪

How is this therapeutic process especially pastoral in nature? Viktor Frankl has written that within the framework of psychotherapy, the methodology and technique applied at any given time is the least effective of all; "rather it is the human relationship between (therapist) and patient which is determining."[30] To the extent that the therapist is concerned with the child and the parents' real selves, and is willing to engage them in a genuine relationship of mutuality, the therapist is healing the whole person. To this extent, the therapist attempts what Clinebell has called the holistic approach to pastoral care and counseling, since such an approach "sees us human beings as possessing a wealth of undiscovered and undeveloped strengths, assets, and resources."[31] These are discovered in the "story" which is shared in the therapeutic study.

This attempt to enable each counselee to become whole reflects the Church's mission to liberate and empower. Spiritual wholeness is at its center. By receiving the elements of the story—with its brokenness and pain—the therapist offers the opportunity for healing the true self. What Clinebell calls the "six dimensions" of the whole person are affected by the broken, wounded state, and so all six are healed through enlivening the mind, revitalizing the body, renewing and enriching relationships, deepening the relationship with nature, and growing in relationship to significant institutions which results hopefully in deepening the counselee's relationship with God.[32]

The child, more than any other client or patient, demands to be dealt with in his or her uniqueness and not as a problem. In order to reach the level of mutuality where healing is effected, the therapist must engage and risk himself or herself as a person. He or she helps the child make sense of the story which best expresses who and what the child is. At the same time, the therapist enters the child's story as an important attachment.

Chapter Six illustrates through three case studies the way children struggled with the meaning and value of significant attachments, separations and losses. The therapeutic techniques of symbolizing through various art forms and through story-telling help elucidate, clarify and interpret their story. During therapy there is a conscious effort not to impose an interpretation on the work of the child. Sometimes children themselves interpret their own productions. These creative productions stand on their own and tell the story of the relationships and feelings about others and self.

It is in the significant attachment to the therapist, not in some magic quality of the production of art and symbol alone, that the healing takes place. By traveling the risky path of attachment, separation and loss, the therapist is not only an instrument of healing but is himself or herself healed. The gift to the child is not only a richer, more complete, more complex and unified story but the therapist's own self. Both realities are operative in curing or healing. As in healing miracles of Jesus, not only release from affliction is offered, but the very person of the one mediating the cure. In the cure of the man born blind (Jn 9), Jesus offers himself as well as sight. In this story a cure is effected at considerable price for both the blind man, his parents and Jesus himself. The therapeutic process involves similar risks.

THE ATTACHMENT CYCLE AND THERAPY:
Three Case Illustrations

Introductory Remarks:
The Healing Cycle in Therapy ■ ■

■ We have seen that conceiving of psychological growth as taking place within cycles of attachments, separations and losses has important implications for a definition of health and psychological maturity as well as psychopathology. The latter, we saw, may be conceived of as an arrest or distortion in the ASL-R cycle where human relationships offering care and security are not or were not forthcoming.

Focusing on the reality of the person-in-relationship also helps us appreciate that psychic healing and wholeness is a restoration of the normal cycle which relatedness entails. A restoration of health in relationships necessitates the involvement of a therapist willing to enter into a relationship characterized by dialogue, care and self-communication. The therapist helps to restore health and wholeness by the offer of mutuality: "I care enough to take on your issues. Your pain does not frighten me. I accept these as my pain and my issues." The three cases examined in this chapter reveal aspects of the therapeutic process and the special relationship between therapist and client.

To a large degree, the healing process does not differ in cases involving either children or adults. The therapist provides an environment of care such that both therapist and client may come to perceive their own relationship as important. The therapist's monitoring of the client's journey of discovery enables the client to take risks that lead to insights into the nature of the unhealthy or stalled relationship. This allows for the healing of the self which has been damaged or thwarted sometimes quite early on in life. The client's self, hidden for protection against the onslaught of anxious sentiments of unworthiness or inadequacy, experiences a rebirth through healing.

In the case of children and families, the journey into relationship with the therapist and the examination of distorted past relationships is full of hazards and obstacles. It is also full of spontaneous and happy moments of growth. These moments, however, demand a price on the part of both therapist and client. So, in providing a "holding environment," the therapist offers a self. Beyond a concern for health and autonomy, the therapist has in mind the creation of a relationship offering mutual affirmation and acceptance, a model for future relationships.

As an attachment bond develops, a struggle against over-dependence follows naturally in the therapeutic relationship. The need on the client's part for the respect and love of the therapist and the felt need on the part of the therapist for the acceptance and love of the client produce this struggle. Pcychologists, beginning with Freud, have often down played the implications of this and in some cases have flatly rejected an understanding of the therapeutic process as healing. Rather, some have stressed the analytical nature of the encounter, paying little attention to those important conditions which foster healing, such as the crucial element of "care."

Margaret Mahler's work with children and her insights into the separation-individuation process helps us delineate the way attachments, separations and losses are important aspects of all relationships where care produces genuine growth. Those "phases," as she calls them, ought to be evident in the processes whereby two individuals become agents of one another's growth. Although the child may be the obvious beneficiary of the healing process in therapy, just as the child is the obvious beneficiary of the care given by parents, there is an important, often less obvious benefit which accrues to the therapist and care-giver. Therapists are healed in the therapeutic process, just as parents mature in raising their children. The child is mother and father to his or her parents. The three case studies which follow provide us with evidence of how the healing process works in the ASL-R cycle which occurs in therapy. Since the drawings of the children are used to illustrate this process, a brief word about the use of projective drawings in therapy follows.

The Use of Projective Drawings ▪▪

Collin and Hayes observe that the use of art in therapy helps promote greater awareness on the part of both the therapist and the client. They feel that artistic productions promote in the client "what it means to be human."[1] Counseling is both an art and a science, believes Gladding, and as such the artistic dimension must be taken more seriously, especially with regard to helping counselors appreciate the artistic nature of the process of coming to understand and help another as well as how to use artistic methods.[2] The systematic use of the arts in counseling is a fairly recent phenomenon, but one which is growing and becoming more widely accepted as useful in helping the therapist to understand the affective and cognitive life of the client, and as an aid in the healing process itself.

Those who write on the subject of art and the use of projective drawings fall into three major camps. Some proponents of projective drawings stress the diagnostic usefulness of this art. Others believe that art within the confines of the therapeutic situation is a means of communication between client and therapist, and a few stress the healing properties of art done for its own sake.

A great deal of the research on the use of projective drawings in therapy is summed up by DiLeo whose books have helped establish the objective validity of projective drawings, along with the work of Goodenough, Landgarten and Kellogg.[3] DiLeo believes that children draw what they have seen, what they remember at the moment and how they feel about what they are trying to depict. He lists six answers to the question: What do children draw? When given the freedom and the "holding environment," children draw (1) what is important to them, predominantly people, then animals, horses, trees; (2) some, but not all, of what is known about the object; (3) what is remembered at the time; (4) the idea colored by feelings; (5) what is seen; (6) inner reality, not an optical one. To DiLeo, children are "expressionists."[4] The object selected for representation serves as a catalyst for expressing feelings and ideas. Children make sense of the world, and thus of their histories, by languaging it and/or by picturing it. Stories and artistic expressions are windows into the inner lives of children. They are also mirrors, reflecting the way the world is being internally processed. Those feelings and issues which do not find verbal expressions find their way into art.

Drawing and story-telling is an important way to establish a rapport between therapist and client, for they communicate on several levels at once. Learning to appreciate and understand the meaning of the communications is a matter of appreciating and understanding the particular ways an individual child has learned to express those feelings and opinions. This longitudinal approach is superior to one which takes an overly analytical approach to each single drawing. Over time, in other words, one learns a great deal about the particular "language" of the child's drawings and artistic productions. How the themes, particular use of colors, objects and medium change can tell a great deal about what is happening in the child from one session to the next. Drawings, over time, express a subtlety of intellect and affect that go beyond what verbal expression can capture. Art has a power and a freedom lacking in the verbal communication of children.

While some therapists concentrate on details of the drawing such as the position of a figure, the relative size and number of details, and the use or absence of color, it is always important to place these details in the context of that which is already known about the child. His or her history, level of intelligence, exposure to stimulating or arid environments, help weigh each evaluation. When placed alongside a series of drawings or artistic productions which are produced over the weeks of therapy, and, it must be remembered for a particular person, the therapist, these drawings say something about the nature of the relationship which has been created. These are specific communications, in other words, with a specific person and may reflect the levels of trust and feelings for or against the therapist. Children draw their inner world but they are influenced by the person with whom they are communicating. This issue has not been addressed in the literature to any great extent.

We have said that art in therapy has been described as useful for several reasons, especially as an aid in diagnosis and a device for communication. But a third approach to understanding projective value of art in therapy is its healing properties. Only Kivnick and Erikson have proposed, in any forceful manner, that art can heal in and of itself and so suggest that aside from its value as a therapeutic technique it "stands on its own" in some unique way. They outline seven specific properties of art which make healing possible. As an "unconscious wellspring of creativity," artistic activity heals because it helps tip a balance toward the positive side of several opposing tendencies. This positive pole, condition or attitude, as they call it, needs restoration in those experiencing mental difficulties, anxiety and confusion. The seven are identified as follows: *activity* vs. *inactivity* (art is an active engagement with the environment); *imagination* vs *over-concreteness* (art requires that imaginative faculties be exercised, a crucial ingredient for health); *sensory expression* vs. *strict verbal expression* (in art more of the senses are exercised); *lawfulness* vs. *unpredictability* (the artist must acknowledge that order, symmetry and planning are important in one way or another when producing something as a communication of inner feelings and opinions); *concentration* vs. *distraction* (when drawing or telling a story, for example, the artist must attend to details, plan and select and thus in some way tame the mind); *catharis* vs. *inhibition* (those who are especially unable to use language are able to act out in ways that express feelings which are deep and powerful, and find in art the chance to express themselves in socially acceptable ways); *mastery* vs. *helplessness* (art, because it is a production requiring all the above, helps build a sense of accomplishment and power).[5]

By promoting the positive side of these seven opposite poles, the effects of ill health are nullified and wounds to the psyche are healed. These two authors conclude their discussion of the healing properties of art by saying: "We believe that in a setting in which people are encouraged to engage in art activities, almost everyone, if not absolutely everyone, can experience the unique sense of healing along with the satisfactions embodied in working creatively with materials."[6]

So, art has several important contributions to make to the therapeutic process—as a diagnostic aid, as a device for projecting feelings as well as "visions" of the inner and outer world, and as a healing activity in and of itself. In the cases which we will now see, the artistic productions contributed in all three ways to the therapeutic goals. The artistic productions are, however, most valuable when seen as a chronicle of the healing process and as a communication to one who is trusted and valued. The child's art helps both a self and another, the therapist, who may be described as the "holding" person. It helps us assess, evaluate and monitor the effects of care or carelessness on the child by those to whom the child is attached, from whom the child must separate, or whom the child has lost. Taken together, they form a pictorial story of the healing process itself.

Case 1: Henry (age 4 1/2), "On Whom Can I Rely?" ▪▪

The case of "Henry" is an example of a child's struggle to come to terms with the loss of a parent. Henry's father died when he was two years old. His treatment in therapy illustrates, among other things, the attempt of Henry, as with any child in therapy, to find healing. Such healing occurs when the therapist is willing to receive the story of the child's difficulty, hurt and loss. Henry's drawings and art productions in therapy reflect the process whereby he endeavored to make sense of his life as well as hand over to another his confusion and pain. (Aspects of the family story have been changed in minor ways to protect the identity of these individuals but not to alter the significance of the data.)

The drawings which Henry produced during the sessions give dramatic evidence of the internal process of meaning-making which is a crucial part of therapy. Like those drawings produced by William, or those of Agnes, they are the vehicles for expression of feelings and ideas by clients whose capacity for dealing in abstract concepts is limited or non-existent. Nevertheless, if the imagination is given freedom, space, and allowed to work with minimal interference from the outside, then a kind of dialogue begins to take place. This dialogue occurs, as we discussed in an earlier section, not only between the child and the drawings but between the child and the therapist through the use of the drawings. Such non-verbal communication helps facilitate the healing process.

Henry was 4 1/2 at the time of his referral. He had been acting up in pre-school and had bitten another child. This was the second time Henry had misbehaved in this way. Since children do not bite after about two to three years of age (hands replace the mouth as the source of and means of aggression), his pre-school teachers insisted that he see someone.

Background: Henry was born premature by one month. At the time when his mother discovered she was pregnant, his father was diagnosed as having a type of terminal cancer. Henry's premature birth was precipitated by a major attack, the first, of the bone cancer's debilitating effects. During the course of therapy—fifteen sessions with Henry and five with his mother—it was learned that Henry's father was home the entire time of his first two years of life. Henry's father never discussed his illness, except to complain of its painful consequences. His mother cared for both child and husband as the needs of both mounted. Finally, when Henry was about two years of age his father's condition had deteriorated to the point of hospitalization. He died after two months of hospitalization, never having said goodbye to Henry nor to his wife.

Diagnosis: Henry seemed to be suffering from a delayed grief reaction, even though he was only two when his father died. His vivid memories of his father "walking on the wall," that is, holding onto the wall to get to the bathroom, or of the family watching TV together, until Henry could no longer sit on the bed with his father, indicate that Henry had been "working" to remember and hold on to these events. Thus, he must have "languaged" them afterward. For Henry's mother, the difficult situation, especially her husband's refusal to discuss his impending death, and the "ruining" of this special event, the birth of their first child, indicate that her own grief reaction was complicated by the ambiguous relationships which must have developed over the course of her son's first two years of life and her husband's last two.

The Process of Therapy   ▪▪

During the initial phases of therapy, Henry painted rainbows. (Drawing A-1) He was immediately at ease in the new surroundings and displayed a remarkable understanding that the relationship was to be something special. His mother had prepared him by telling him that he could speak with the therapist about any

Pictures of rainbows dominate the first sessions. (A-1).

topic and that sessions would be full of play and fun activities. She also explained that his biting at school had something to do with the reason he was coming to visit with this "new friend." In addition, she herself said that she would be visiting with this new friend once in a while.

After several weeks, Henry began to relax and then one day painted a picture of a "collapsed rainbow." (Drawing A-2) He seemed ready to reveal a well-hidden sadness. Shortly after this, he wanted to make a snowman, or "snowlady" as he called it. In the next session, he decided to make a clay mouse. This was inspired by the story of an incident at home. He explained that his mother had killed a little mouse which had been found inside the trash can. The death of the mouse made him very sad. It was at this time that Henry began a serious struggle with his work in ther-

As therapy progressed, the "rainbow collapsed." (A-2).

apy. Some sessions were full of resistances—projects begun and destroyed before completion. There were displays of fatigue and impatience. In one session Henry wanted to write "no" continously on construction paper.

Shortly after this he was asked if he would prefer to sit next to the therapist. Since Henry was uncomfortable with being held, it was unusual for him to seek close physical proximity. From the time of his second birthday and especially since the death of his father, Henry's mother believed he had little "apparent" need for physical contact. This was not in actuality the case. The child was hungry for affection and warmth. While on the therapist's lap he drew a picture which he explained as he went along. (Drawing A-3) A man ("a dad" he called it) in a boat jumps out of the boat into the water. He swims across the water to a shore and then climbs

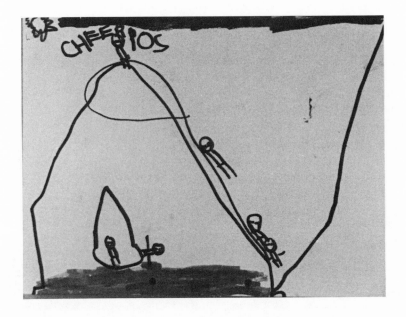

Henry's drawing of a "dad" saying goodbye." (A-3).

a mountain with the aid of a strong rope which leads him to the top. Then the man said "cheerios," a word he apparently associated with "goodbye." Since he could not spell the word he asked the therapist to spell it out. When the session ended, Henry jumped down to meet his mother. This was the first time that he left a session without complaining that it was too short.

In the meantime, sessions with his mother attempted to get her to examine her relationship with her husband and especially his sickness and death—all of which occurred at the time when she was having her first and only child. During the initial interview, she attested that having Henry was the happiest time of her life. Later on in her consultation sessions, she stated that she felt disappointment and even anger over the fact that her husband's condition deteriorated from the time of Henry's conception, and that his death when Henry was only two was experienced as both a relief and as unfair in that it deprived her and her son of a real family life. There were then many mixed and uncertain feelings and reactions. Her husband's inability to speak about his dying and his own mother's reaction, often extremely dramatic, made those final two years confusing and painful for Henry's mother. Since her husband's death was experienced as a relief, something which she could admit to only after the fourth session, her anger had been mixed with guilt.

While needing to come to terms with her husband's death for herself, Henry's mother, at the same time, needed to allow her son, Henry, the opportunity to do the same. Her complaint was often that her son remembered too much and that he seemed to carry his father inside him, that he was already older than he should be. This woman was able to begin her grief work, talking to her mother-in-law, her boyfriend, and the therapist, as well as speaking directly to Henry about his father for the first time. Once she heard that Henry had already said good-bye to his father, an interpretation of the picture he had drawn, she felt a kind of permission to settle some things herself regarding his memory.

The fact that Henry could begin his grief work but could not complete it without her was dramatically portrayed in the next series of drawings (A-4 and A-5). These drawings were of a boy trapped in a tower, in a castle surrounded by a moat with a drawbridge. These were painful pictures for him. He often cried while doing them and insisted that the therapist help with the drawings because he could not do them alone.

During this period Henry's mother struggled with the idea of speaking with her son about his father. She had always hesitated to do so because her in-laws, she said, talked about him and because she believed (as do many therapists) that Henry was too young to mourn. However, once she began discussing what Henry's father was like, the relationship between mother and son began to change. The next sessions were lighter. Henry stopped the tower drawings and began drawing squares, flags, and other designs of wholeness (A-6).

With this we initiated the termination stage by explaining to Henry that he did not need to come as often and that our sessions would be further and further apart, first every two weeks, then

Towers and moats with drawbridges and boys trapped within them. (A-4 and A-5).

once a month or every three weeks. He resisted the suggestion and pretended not to hear until the final sessions drew near. For his final session, Henry drew a woman with large feet (A-7), as if to say: "Mom is more stable, more secure; her feet are on the ground." He accepted the termination of therapy with sadness but said he would make a gift and send it. The gift was a photo of him and his mother in a hand-made card.

Besides seeing the healing process documented in Henry's art, we can trace the stages of therapy in terms which parallel Mahler's separation-individuation process. The case example of Henry mirrors this process and in so doing attests to the rhythm inherent in relationships which facilitate real growth and acknowledge the necessity of negotiating painful separations and losses.

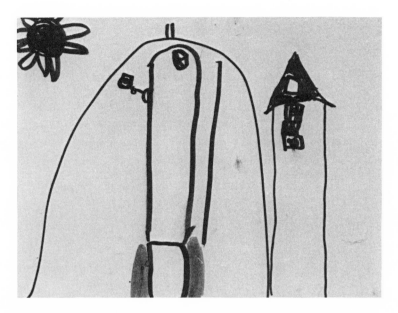

(A-5).

The therapeutic cycle traces the separation-individuation process as detailed in the table on pp. 130–133, but two additional points are worth noting. First, the healing process is completed after the child has experienced himself or herself as successful without the therapist. In other words, the cycle must be completed: the loss of the therapist as a special support must be mourned, and this will take place during termination and after. Second, healing is effected at the level of the self in the therapeutic process. The necessary condition is the genuine interest of another self (therapist) and the experience of mutual affirmation, that is, the chance to give and to receive love. Therapy involves a building and fostering of self-esteem which comes from healing experienced foremost as acceptance.

Flags and squares: symbols of wholeness and completion. (A-6).

Four Important Conclusions ▪▪

If we examine or describe the therapeutic healing process in such terms, we are better able to understand the rhythm of closeness and distance which occurs with clients during the course of therapy. We also glimpse the internal struggle of the client. The client needs to move close and then move away, resisting, then checking back for confirmation. Henry's struggle is mirrored both in his artistic productions and in his attachment to the therapist. His attachment to the therapist allows him the freedom to do the grief work while still "waiting" for his mother's acceptance and confirmation. In the end, Henry is better able to attach to his mother and to other people, such as her boyfriend, who also noted a positive difference in their relationship over time.

A mom who is well-grounded: we'll be OK. (A-7).

In the light of this, it is more accurate to describe Henry's therapy as leading to a more mature dependence than independence. He gave the impression, in fact, at the beginning of therapy of being too independent, of being "a little adult," as his mother called him, but one who "bites" when frustrated because he had never really been a child. No doubt he had heard many times, especially from his father's family: you have to be a little man and take care of your mother now that your father is sick, or, later on, now that your dad has gone.

Second, Henry used symbolic representations to display for both the therapist and for himself his sentiments, beliefs, moods. Without more sophisticated communication skills, and even with such language, words could not capture the fullness of the child's experiences and feelings as well as do the artistic creations (such as a "collapsed rainbow"). Ambiguous feelings, like the relationships that produce them, cannot be so precisely given or named. The ambiguous relationship he had with his father makes the coming to terms more difficult and more complex. The story of a man, "a dad," climbing a mountain or a boy trapped in a tower better capture the "meanings" of these experiences for this child in vivid pictures that communicate as they heal.

Third, Henry's wounded self is directly tied to his mother's wounded self. When he heals, she will heal, and vice versa. As we saw, an exact paralleling of their healing work need not occur as long as the therapist is able to "hold" one or both individuals in some sense. The therapist helps wait out the timing, then gives the permission and translates that permission in the child. Had the two not come to some resolution or initiation of the grieving proc-

■ ■ ■ ■ ■ ■ ■ ■ ■ ■

Table 2: *The Attachment, Separation, Loss and Rebirth Cycle in Therapy*

Stage	Characteristics	Therapeutic Technique/Process
One: "Normal Autism"	Child is aloof, guarded, cautious, withdrawn.	Introduction to process and place
	Child shares small amounts of information	Finding common interests
		Determination of level of competencies, e.g., language of feelings,

comprehension, artistic interest, talents

Determination of form of symbolic expression—toys/play, games/painting, etc.

Establish understanding and rapport with parent(s), teachers—fact finding.

Two: "Symbiotic"	Rhythm of interaction established	Establish pattern of work, and symbolic expression
	Child cherishes time together	Explore personal topics, issues
	Treatment of therapist as equal, i.e., repeats many of the problems, with parents, peers, in projects done "together"	More of a rhythm apparent in togetherness and in quiet time together, an important element in healing work
		Importance of therapist will be demonstrated in the "gifts"

	A sharing of activity, of memories of concerns occurs in therapy	With parents and teachers, exploration of ways to change, improve environment

Three: "Hatching and Rapprochement"	Continuation of stable and predictable environment, conditions	Maintain parameters of meeting and discussion
		Therapist moves back and forth between active and passive interaction
	Child takes some risks in the relationship; may refuse, ignore, withdraw	Occasional exploration of "meanings" of art, of behavior, etc.
	Child concentrates on self, in presence of therapist	Parents (and teachers?) begin to express anxiety and sense child's health and other issues (theirs?)
	Child sometimes bored, i.e., depressed, fearful	

Four: "Separation and Individuation"	Child senses and discusses successes	Continue with stable sessions, environment

	Child notes differences between self and others	Review successes, differences
		Discuss "others" in more objective fashion
	Very matter-of-fact, frank in conversation	Projects in art more detailed and deliberate
	Intense in work and play	Prepare for termination—"a vote for confidence"
	May make gift of art in specific fashions	
	Plays with new sense of freedom	

Five: "Termination and Mature Interdependence"	Some re-enactment old issues, styles of interaction with therapist	Identify successes
		Identify regressive behavior and feelings of anger, frustration
	Sadness over loss, even anger	Discuss meaning of therapy, conversations
	Show of affection, celebration	Exchange gifts

ess, Henry, we might speculate, would have been inordinately tied to his mother, or overly "distant." He could have moved away from her into an emotional independence and perhaps an isolation which is not conducive for individuation.

Finally, Henry's pictures, which depict his identification with the mouse that is crushed, the man crossing a river and climbing a mountain, the boy stuck in the tower, and the lady with firmly planted feet, form a powerful narrative piece. They are images of his larger story which he can carry as part of his unique identity. Regardless of whether they are forgotten or remembered, they will affect his self-perception as they contribute to his self-cohesion. In this healing, Henry's preoccupation with being an adult and with holding on to memories of his father receded into the background. He was once again free to struggle with attachment, separation and loss issues without being unduly hampered by fear and anxiety.

Healing in the Interpsychic and Intrapsychic Spheres ■■

An assumption runs through the previous chapters concerning the locus of the healing process. Putting this in the form of a question, we might ask: Does healing take place within the child, that is, intrapsychically, or does it take place between the therapist and the child or between the child and others, that is, interpsychically? How ought we to understand, then, the focus of therapy? Case material indicates that healing occurs on several levels simultaneously. That is, children and adults are healed internally when they are healed in their interpersonal relationships. Several factors or forces operate at once.

Traditionally, there has been a division among therapists on this issue. One of the leading theorists of child and family therapy, Rudolf Dreikurs, has written: "Discussion and therapy deal with the dynamic that operates within the family. Since the problems of the child express his interpersonal conflict, the counselor deals with all members of the family who unwittingly take part in the conflict."[7] Dreikurs was influential in steering child therapy in the direction of interpersonal issues and problems by stressing Adlerian concepts of power, influence, control.

Others, such as Jungians, have chosen to concentrate on the inner world of the child and the healing process which is, these theorists hold, intrapsychic in nature since psychological problems are essentially matters of internal states and conflicts.[8]

Our model has, on the other hand, attempted to steer an even course between the two positions. Work with children and families is truly pastoral and truly effective if it recognizes that issues represent both interpersonal concerns and wounds to the child's internal psychic life. Healing must address both spheres.

Ackerman's important book, *Treating the Troubled Family*, helped the therapy profession clarify the aims of work with families with identified problems.[9] The focus and primary task of such therapy must be the conflict within and between family members. The uncovering of individual and group issues means that each family member must be given his or her own freedom, encouragement and time. The process with each will differ depending on accessibility and how amenable each is to constructing a relationship with someone able to help. Extreme care and caution must be exercised on the part of helping individuals not to interfere with the way needs for inclusion, belonging, self-control, affection, privacy, the practice of autonomy and the movement toward mature dependence are met by the family system.

In light of this, the therapist is confronted with three distinct dilemmas. He or she must assertain the extent and nature of the identified problem. Is the identified problem (person) the "real" problem? The therapist must seek to discover the seriousness and depth of the problem(s). And, finally, the therapist will need to know to what extent the enactment or mode chosen for revealing the problem is symbolic of deeper unresolved issues in those family members not identified as problems. As therapy progresses with one or several members of a family, the answers to these questions will emerge and may change.

Case 2: William (age 7), "Is the World a Safe Place?" ■■

The case of William and his family is illustrative of the many levels and aspects of the healing process. It demonstrates, too, that healing within one fosters a healing between and among family members. So restoring health to one family member is dependent on the relationship with the therapist and on healing taking place within others who form the primary family unit.

William was in therapy for a total of two years. The reason for referral was his poor school performance. At the time he began therapy he was seven and had been acting up in class and at home. School officials felt he needed psychological attention or would have to be left back at the end of the first grade. In the initial session, his mother indicated that her husband had been drinking too much and that this, in her judgment, was directly related to William's misbehavior. William's father had recently been laid off of his job as a prison guard after an unfortunate incident in which he was overcome by several inmates. This resulted in a bout of depression and excessive use of alcohol.

Since William's father was opposed to family therapy, William's mother determined that therapy should concentrate on helping William overcome his own difficulties, boost his poor self-esteem, and put an end to his teasing and negative behavior at school and at home with his one sister, one year older than him.

We agreed that things would not change appreciably until William's father was also in some form of treatment. Yet, working with William might be the catalyst for such treatment. That is, in fact, what happened. About two months after therapy began with William and regular sessions with his mother, his father was admitted to a residential treatment program for alcoholism and depression. Getting help from someone outside the family became suddenly a reasonable activity. When he returned home after six weeks he asked to be included in sessions discussing William's progress. In the meantime, a battery of learning disabilities tests was given to William, and these revealed the need for tutoring in reading, a problem contributing to his own poor self-image and negative behavior at school.

During the course of the sessions with William's parents it became apparent that each was struggling with issues directly related to his or her own upbringing. William's mother had been raised in a quiet home where conflict was not dealt with openly. Her own mother had made sure that the children never fought or disturbed their father, so the siblings learned to find outlets for aggression outside the family or held it inside.

William's father, on the other hand, had experienced a very painful family history. His own mother was cold and unable to show affection. Over the years she had become obsessed with order and neatness and threatened to send her son to boarding school if he misbehaved—a threat she ultimately carried out. His own school background was a disaster and his ability to control his anger and its expression had never been developed, leading to his problem with alcoholism. It became obvious, especially to his wife, that his marriage was a desperate attempt to find the secure, accepting environment of which he had been deprived. His children's imperfections and his own anxiety over being a parent without having been himself "parented" overwhelmed him as much as his failures at work. The inability to control anger, like his wife's inability to express it, was the result of learned patterns of behavior and early childhood wounds.

Such a family situation put William in a more vulnerable position than his sister who identified readily with her mother— keeping calm, internalizing any frustrations and channeling energy into work at school. He became terrified of his father's angry outbursts and thus had never succeeded in building a cohesive self, a positive identity, or productive work habits.

Progress in Therapy ■■

This family presents a variety of issues and problems for consideration. The process of therapy with William is worth examining because it illustrates the way his healing and growth was tied to that of other members of the family, and concomitantly with his relationship with the therapist.

The first phase of the process dealt with determining the nature, depth and scope of the issues affecting William and his place in the family pathology. The two drawings from this period, B-1 and B-2, are instructive. The first, from one of the first therapy sessions, is a family drawing. "Mom" is the only human figure. She is walking two pets—one of them scurrying up the tree, the other on a leash. Dad is absent. William identified himself as the one who cannot be controlled. His sister is "tied" to his mother. As a portrait, it represents quite accurately the dynamics operating in this family.

A family drawing: mom, with two pets, one attached and the other un-controllable. (B-1, above).
This drawing was produced early on in therapy: it depicts a ship at war with its surroundings. (B-2).

The second drawing produced during the third session is a battle scene on a ship. Men are walking the plank, birds have snatched up fish, and ropes form a kind of prison-like grill on board. The drawing may be understood as representative of both his inner psychic life and the outer, social environment, the state of the family. As with most children, the drawings were not discussed. Ability to express these concepts in pictures during this first stage of therapy is itself a remarkable achievement. Allowing such pictures to speak for themselves encourages free expression and relieves the child of the burden of interpretation.

With a relationship established between therapist and child, a second stage of the healing process ensued. This stage involved William's expressions about himself more directly. Without being asked to draw himself, pictures which represented his own feel-

Feelings of omnipotence compensate for feelings of inferiority. (B-3).

ings of grandiosity—a sign often of a fragmented or damaged ego—of anger, frustration or loneliness, were produced. Pictures B-3 and B-4 are representative of this period which lasted throughout the time his father was in residential treatment for alcoholism and depression. A superman or superboy flying off to the moon (B-3) and a sea lion stranded on a rock at sea (B-4) capture these feelings and worries. In our discussions, William shifted from statements of helplessness (I can't do such and such at school) to grandiosity (I'm the only one who . . .).

His father's interest in cooperating with the therapy and his concern that his son achieve success in school initiated the third stage of healing. A relative stability at home allowed William to turn his attentions toward his social feelings. He fought regularly in therapy sessions as he did with his classmates at school. Meet-

Feelings of being alone and stranded emerge in the second phase as mutuality in relationship with the therapist grows. (B-4).

---

ings with his parents and with his teacher focused on strategies for dealing with his poor self-control and his work habits. This difficult but important period was often represented in therapy by pictures of dragons and dinosaurs spitting fire (B-5), or by lions devouring lambs or some other helpless animal. The world as a menacing place, a dangerous place, was depicted in his art work. Over time, these feelings subsided. Since it was extremely difficult for his father to tolerate such rage or for his mother to appreciate on a conscious level these sentiments, William needed a safe place to express them where they would be acknowledged, accepted, and valued.

Stage four in the healing process was directly related to progress in school and to his father's own gains in a work rehabilitation program. William focused on his peer relationships, quite

Here the monster directs his rage at the outside world. (B-5).

normal for his age group, and on control of his outbursts when frustrated. His father expressed his pride at William's academic improvements and practiced controlling his own temper at home, perhaps learning from his son. Two drawings selected from this period of therapy, B-6 and B-7, illustrate William's inner and outer state. In B-7 two ferocious dinosaurs are in battle but seem to be at a stand-off. In B-8, however, the dinosaur which seems to represent archaic, powerful, mysterious, oversized feelings is given words; he identifies himself as a "good dinosaur." It appears from such drawings that William has begun to accept his feelings and control his actions, aggressions and fears. With that a more positive self-image began to develop.

Progress had been made on several fronts in William's life—improved school and work habits, better relationships with his

Helplessness and fear—both powerful feelings and lack of control of them—are expressed in this drawing: a lion has attacked a helpless lamb. This is a representation of feelings internal and feelings about the world. (B-6).

peers and his sister, less fear and more involvement with his father. This led to healing in the interpsychic and intrapsychic levels, and thus the process of termination began. This fifth and final stage involved demonstrations of resentment against the therapist, and an attempt to reclaim the need for therapy by a series of failures in school and renewed fighting with his sister at home. Once these were discussed and identified as possible reactions to loss, they stopped. His art work in the final months is indicative of the inner control, peace and safety which William experienced in both his internal psychic life and in his interpersonal relationships. For example, B-9 was produced one month before the termination date. It is a horse, corralled but free to roam within its borders. And, the final drawing in therapy, which William said was "his best," B-10 is of a dove descending to earth. A mountain, sea,

Powerful internal and external forces are here depicted as at a stand-off. (B-7).

clear sky and a bright sun represent all the elements, a world which is complete and in harmony. There are no ferocious beasts, no underwater or land fights. A kind of controlled freedom permeates these pictures, indicating health and wholeness.

Discussion ■ ■

In his book, *The Healing Dialogue in Psychotherapy*, Friedman writes: "Psychotherapy in our age has been guilty of one of the great violations of reality in that it has often focused so much on the inner psychic world—the neurosis or complex of the person—and has tended to treat parents, family and culture as psychic symbols rather than as the concrete social context of the

Some overpowering and uncontrollable feelings may actually be good:
"This is a good dinosaur." (B-8).

---

person's day-to-day existence."[10] Healing comes in dialogue,
Friedman notes. It comes in the meeting of two persons who explore the concrete realities of their world.

The case of William and his family demonstrates that well-
being is achieved when difficult attachments are negotiated, when
environmental influences are corrected, and when creative energies are addressed and harnessed for their healing potentiality.
Healing must occur on several levels at once since past and present come to bear on the helplessness and hopelessness expressed
in negative behavior. The therapist reawakens seeds of hope buried, as in the case of William's family, under mounting pressures
from school, job and home. The opportunity to express negative
as well as hopeful feelings and beliefs in the safety of the thera-

Freedom means roaming within appropriate boundaries. (B-9).

peutic environment is itself nurturing. By fostering collaboration and by a willingness to enter the story of each family member, the therapist helps create a new family story. The gift of patient waiting and acceptance models for the family what individual members can give to one another. It is then not the skill of the therapist as much as the person which becomes the crucial ingredient in the healing process. Our next and last example helps to illustrate this final point.

Healing and the Problem of Transference/Countertransference ▪▪

We have seen in the previous two cases that the healing process is complex, occurring on many levels and influenced by a va-

145

The final picture: a world harmonious, in order. (B-10).

riety of factors. "Techniques" such as artistic productions, interpretation, consultation, changing the environment and so on are involved, but play a supportive role. Physical healing offers a good analogy. A wound is healed when medical procedures, plus hygiene, diet and a caring environment, combine to foster the healing process in one willing to place his or her condition in the hands of another.

To a large extent, psychic healing is the result of a host of factors within a "therapeutic" encounter between people. It occurs due to a specific relationship between client and therapist. For when a bond has been created that allows another to experience genuine worth, it also allows the other the freedom to move out, to separate and to discover something new about the self experienced as more intact. Moreover, in the experience of having survived even and especially the loss of a relationship in its present or old form, some new more cohesive self is formed from the ashes of the older relationship. Friedman, in his investigation of healing in therapy, was forced to conclude that healing involved, at bottom, "an existential grace." That is, it is something ultimately unexplainable. It is essentially a gift, from therapist to client, and from the client to the client's self.

The final issue which deserves some discussion is that of transference in therapy. Both countertransference and transference have been, since Freud, recognized as pivotal for understanding the therapeutic process. What then is the role of the therapist, especially the therapist's ego, and how does the therapist serve as catalyst for making the issues in relationship development the central force in healing? For, as Buber has said: it is not the therapist's superior technique that in the final analysis cures. It is, rather, the therapist's self which does so, and serves as the instrument for the restorative process.[11] The case of Agnes may help demonstrate several points.

Case 3: Agnes (age 8), "Who Can Tolerate My Neediness?" ▪▪

Agnes was referred for therapy when her second grade teacher determined that her classroom behavior had become so disruptive that she was learning very little and disturbing all her classmates at the same time. After a determination that her problems did not stem from learning difficulties and that the acting-out behavior was evidence of some other adjustment problem, her parents agreed to a therapeutic intervention.

Her parents explained that she had been difficult to handle since the birth of her brother four years ago. It seems that most relatives and teachers quite naturally liked her younger brother's disposition and resented Agnes' neediness, complaining and disobedience.

Sibling rivalry, a normal and natural phenomenon, can become debilitating when siblings perceive that the specialness of certain attachment relationships has been unfairly interrupted and destroyed, or that a home is not big enough to handle all of the child's needs. The child experiences these needs as overwhelming and unmanageable. The acting-out behavior, then, is a

Agnes' world: split, uneven, with an intruding sun. (C-1).

desperate cry for the healing of wounds inflicted by the rupture of an attachment, separation and loss cycle occurring with the birth of the "other" sibling. These children feel overshadowed by one another, locked out, as if their story had been taken over by someone else who has assumed the main character position.

During the initial stages of therapy, Agnes discussed her brother a great deal and was incapable of focusing on school problems such as concentration in school work and cooperation in group activities. When doing pictures of the family, Agnes always began with the younger brother and then proceeded to draw other members of the family, mom and dad. Once she even "forgot" to put herself in the picture until the therapist pointed out this absence. Picture C-1 shows Agnes with her cousins where she is the last and smallest child. C-2 shows her family, with herself

A family drawing: Agnes is last, without arms. (C-2).

to the far right, drawn last, without arms, as if to demonstrate that connections seemed impossible.

During the course of this initial part of the therapy, Agnes often referred to the therapist as a "special friend." In the next period of therapy, when in the company of her "friend," she was able to concentrate on herself and even managed to draw herself with no one else in the picture (C-3).

The security experienced in therapy led to a new phase. In one drawing a cloud has settled on the earth and the flowers are "square." With a growing ability to reflect on her "self," Agnes began to examine her peer relationships and admit that she was, at least in part, responsible for their resentment and her teacher's frustrations. "If the world is collapsing or if it appears mixed-up, I may have something to do with it," may be one way of inter-

Agnes alone. Here she is a flower. (C-3).

preting her drawing. Over time, Agnes felt the need to defend her negative actions and discuss her brother less and less. C-4 shows a drawing from this new phase. It is a scene from school and shows the chaos she experienced there. It was during this period that she asked her teacher if the therapist could be her regular classroom teacher. She even introduced the therapist, who visited her at school, as her "other teacher." As problems began to be ironed out and as progress was made in school behavior through regular consultations with parents and teacher, Agnes experienced success in dealing with others, and sought less often to be the center of attention. C-5 shows her friends at school connected by rainbows, a favorite motif, with Agnes at the end of the rain-

Friends play: Agnes is on a small craft out to sea. (C-4).

bow. Her little brother is sailing out of the picture (her explanation). Agnes recognized her progress as her teacher was able to show her examples of improved behavior and work in class. During the termination period, lasting about two months, she often drew herself with the therapist. In one drawing she said that she thought he was like her father and so she drew him with a hat, explaining that she was well aware that the therapist did not wear a hat but that her father did (C-6).

During the last session she wanted to leave a "portrait" of the two "friends," herself and the therapist. This time, as she began to draw a hat, she stopped herself and said that there should be no hat since the therapist did not wear one. In the final drawing she also placed a tree and a rainbow coming down between the two, symbolizing, perhaps, the fulfillment of her innate hopes and the

As therapy progresses, "little brother" sails out of the picture (lower left hand). (C-5).

growth and development of her "self" (C-7). Agnes stands in this final drawing alongside her special friend, teacher, parent-figure. Before discussing some specifics of this case, a brief overview of transference/countertransference in the pertinent literature might be helpful.

Traditional Approaches to
Transference and Countertransference ■■

Greenson has written perhaps the standard work on the issue of transference.[12] He defined transference as "a special kind of relationship toward a person; a distinctive type of object relations." In therapy, this means that the client projects onto the therapist characteristics which do not befit that person. These

Agnes draws her therapist and herself. The therapist has a hat like dad's. (C-6).

actually apply to another. "Essentially, a person in the present—the therapist—is reacted to as though he were a person in the past." Transference, then, is a "repetition, an error in time, a new addition to an old object relationship." Traditional psychoanalytic therapists see it as an "anachronism" and its chief difficulty lies in its being unconscious in the client.

In other words, the therapist is the screen upon which a client projects his or her fantasies. The archaic material—unresolved issues from the past—becomes for the therapist a clue to the nature of the buried, forbidden, painful or unfulfilled wishes from the client's early object relations.

However, if we accept the fact that accomplishments are intrinsically important because there is an innate need for bonding

The final drawing: Agnes and the therapist separated by a rainbow touching earth. (C-7).

or acceptance, that separation leads to individuation, and that loss and rebirth must be experienced in all important relationships, then the focus need not be on the material which the therapeutic relationship "dredges up," but rather on the relationship's potentiality for offering an experience which is health-giving and therefore enabling in itself. The archaic nature of the material is not so much the issue then as the potential for initiating a different outcome to what might begin as an old pattern of relating to another. This approach puts a more positive light on Greenson and the more traditional understanding of the phenomenon of transference. The same holds true for the countertransference.

Therapists sought to understand themselves so as to approach a client in as "transference-free" a state as possible. And by looking for the countertransference reactions in themselves, they would have information regarding those issues being invoked by the client's transference, as well as their own unacknowledged and unaccepted complexes and difficulties with early object relations.

If the transference reactions of the client are not so much archaic issues as examples of the ever-present need of individuals to be understood in their story, then countertransference can be understood more positively as well. The relationship between therapist and client will eventually be characterized by a measure of dependency since a willingness to be vulnerable involves an expression of need on the part of both. Is this necessarily a "regression"? Rather, it may be useful to see this kind of dependency as normal and healthy, as we have indicated in the previous case examples. For those who have not been able to successfully negotiate relationships which are supportive of mutual and healthy dependence, the therapeutic relationship initiates a corrective process by being one where vulnerability is shared. The therapist uses countertransference "reactions" to discover the client's attachment needs, as well as his or her own.

In summary, the therapist must become aware of the various motives, needs, and roles which emerge in the therapeutic encounter and what these say about his or her own needs and desires. Next, the therapist must see the actual value of such roles, motives and needs. By allowing these to develop, within limits, the therapeutic relationship progresses. How, then, ought we understand the countertransference/transference process?

As indicated in previous chapters, the attachment, separation and loss cycle as "normative" of human relationship processes provides a way of understanding the source of countertransference issues. The way issues and needs emerge in the therapist will be directly related to his or her capacity for negotiating difficult attachments, anxious separations and losses. The therapist will need to ask himself or herself: What has been the quality and the style of attachments in my past and present? How do I react and handle separation when others pull away from me? And how do I accept loss in my life?

The therapist, then, must be honest with himself or herself and face squarely the "parenting" function implicit in the therapeutic relationship. Kohut's description of the role of parents is applicable to the therapist's: it is not so much what parents do that inform the character of the child's self, but what the parents are. A mature, cohesive parental self is needed to support the child in its changing moods and needs.[13] Who the therapist is, not the techniques used, governs success in the healing relationship. And who the therapist is will be largely determined by the history of the attachment-separation-loss and rebirth cycles with key, care-giving individuals.

Kernberg believes that countertransference has been too narrowly defined and opts for a definition which includes what he calls the "broad emotional reaction" of the therapist to the client.[14] This operates on both conscious and unconscious levels. Therefore, when considering the countertransference phenomenon one must consider at least three different relationships at work: the relationship between the ego of the therapist and that of the client, the relationship between the unconscious mind of the client and the conscious mind of the therapist, and the unconscious mind of both the therapist and the client. At all these levels, the therapist and the client are relating and are struggling with the creation of some unique new entity—a unique relationship—where the attachment cycle may unfold.

It is not necessary then to limit the roles of the therapist. As someone in a helping relationship, the therapist seeks to fulfill those roles which are appropriate and necessary. Nor does the therapist need to rule out or count as unimportant or destructive any of the needs which the therapeutic environment brings forward, within limits of reasonable and healthy relating. The therapist's different needs—to interpret, to heal, to control, to parent—can at various times be useful and productive. If the therapist is in touch with what is happening in himself or herself, and is careful to maintain a relationship which helps keep perspective through consultation with another professional, then no single transference issue within either the therapist or the client will become an unhealthy, disabling one.

The important questions are shaped by our personal needs for attachment. To what extent does the therapist acting as parent, for example, facilitate on a temporary basis the attachment process? Does the therapist's desire to be the "good father or mother" hinder him or her from allowing the client the freedom to break away? Are fears of losing the client's approval motivated by fear of letting people become independent? Finally, is the therapist aware of the client's growing independence and ability to function without therapy and so can the therapist initiate the termination process? The case of Agnes has illustrated the way roles differ within therapy itself and the way the transference and countertransference, when tolerated, are used in the process of healing.

Discussion and Conclusion ■■

It now seems reasonable to say that all the roles which Agnes needed of the therapist were legitimate transferences from other relationships. But it would be inaccurate to say that these were inappropriate. They were helpful and non-threatening, and were not debilitating since the therapist saw them as only temporary and in some respect "true." Agnes' therapeutic healing process was enhanced and fostered by these "projections." They were roles which others in her life could not play, her narcissistic needs being too overpowering. Over time, as these needs diminished, she was able to test them out and experience them in the trusting holding environment of the therapist's room.

This example also demonstrates what is implied by mutuality and real dialogue: a response to the dictates of the moment. The therapist does not usurp roles which are inappropriate but accepts the necessary roles—as parent, friend, teacher, for example—and respects the limits of the client's conscious awareness and ability to become aware of how the therapist is being used. This means, then, allowing the client to enter the therapist's own life story by becoming the therapist's "friend," "student," "child," without focusing too narrowly on the meaning of the particular type of relationships. Rather, what matters is the attachment potential implicit in them.

Each of these relationships—parent-child, teacher-student, friend-friend—has within it an implied style and depth of bonding. Consequently, there is an implied understanding that separation and loss will follow and will "cost" each individual some pain. The more inexperienced or needy the client, the more "sloppy" these relationships will become. Rogers called the openness which is needed to be a good therapist an issue of "congruence."[15] This is described as a "fit," that is, a willingness to adjust one's personality, temperament, and roles to those of the client. Over time, as roles change, these two people come to know one another as they truly are. This "knowledge" makes genuine care possible.

Finally, the therapist must be aware of his or her own primitive needs and desires which stem from his or her unique history of attachments and losses. The therapist must know his or her own story so as to recognize the legitimate place or places where the client may rightfully take a part. It is this self-knowledge which opens the way for the client to become, for the therapist, someone who counts.

OVERALL SUMMARY AND CONCLUSIONS

■ The influence of Sigmund Freud on the direction and the underlying assumptions of psychoanalysis and psychotherapy in general cannot be minimized. His legacy is enormous and his ideas pervasive. In one of his last major works, *New Introductory Lectures in Psychoanalysis,* Freud states: "The theory of the instincts is so to say our mythology. Instincts are mythical entities, magnificent in their indefiniteness."[1] He went on to say that the living person is at the command of "two intentions," self-preservation and the preservation of the species, often in direct conflict in other animals, but more subtly so in humans.

As a starting point for understanding the human person, this "mythology" has left us with a dismal picture of the human condition; we are alone and at war with both ourselves and our world. If, as Freud said, the source of instincts is a "state of excitation in the body," and if the aim of instincts is the "removal of that excitation," then humans are forever caught up with their own individual psychic and physical conditions. When speaking of human tenderness in that same essay, Freud took the position that it undoubtedly originates from the source of sexual need and invariably renounces satisfaction, a position he first expounded in *Instincts and Their Vicissitudes,* in 1915.

For close adherents of Freud, there seemed to be no way around this dismal view. It explained both the origin of the need for care and love and the child's ability to do without it in the face of a harsh and cruel world.

Others, with less allegiance to Freud, such as Bowlby and Balint, began noticing that a natural bonding between mother and child was the precursor of the lifelong relational process. An innate instinctual drive for satisfaction of the sexual urge, even when modified by an equally potent ability to forego satisfaction, did not, for Bowlby and Balint at least, account for the two-way attachment process which is visible in human and subhuman species. Freud's instinct paradigm is inadequate, they have proposed, to explain relationships which manifest themselves from the first moments of life, and which can endure when gratification is not possible or unevenly given.

It was Sullivan who attempted the first major shift in the object of study. With him, the focus of attention in psychoanalytic research moved from the individual unconscious and conscious mind to the reality of the interpersonal. Sullivan made his point by stressing that the complete psychic reality to which the theorist and the therapist must pay attention is that which exists between persons who, by their relatedness, actually constitute one another. Interpersonal relations define both the personality and the psyche. The integrity and totality of the person is only visible in the client's interpersonal relationships.

Hoping to produce a purely psychodynamic perception of the person without such a Freudian psychobiological emphasis, Melanie Klein attempted a metapsychology of feelings—or a "mythology" of feelings. Instead of psychobiological stages, she hypothesized phases which grow out of the relationship between mother and child. These "positions," as she called them, help us understand the powerful needs for union and the pain in separation. They introduce into psychoanalytic theory the notion of a rhythm of interaction, the child's concern for what happens in the mother, viewed by Klein as the source of morality, and the constant struggle to understand and master the relational process. The dynamic interaction with and importance of the object, the other, is given serious consideration for the role it plays in the intrapsychic life of the child.

Klein's chief contribution lies in her articulation of the early (primitive) feelings of loyalty, regret, jealousy, fear of loss of the other, and the desire to repair damage done in the relational process. The human person from the beginning embarks on a project of creating healthy relationships due to inborn tendencies toward specific psychic experiences. What is "instinctive" in the child is its turn toward the mother and not a regressive pull toward the chasm of selfish gratification of physical or psychic urges. Klein's later concern is with the emotions of the child and not with drives.

With that historical perspective in place we then examined the critical shift in interest and concern from the solitary individual to the mother-child dyad, that is, to the importance of the role of the object. The new breed of psychoanalytic theorists and researchers, represented here by Mahler, Winnicott and Fairbairn, sketched the rhythmic nature of human interactions and the individuation process. The dynamics of separation anxiety are as much the result of a need for pulling away as they are for mutual dependence in normal and healthy development. By concentrating on the interaction between children and their care-takers, these object relations theorists gave us a sound and positive way of conceiving of maturation as phase-appropriate dependence and mutual concern for autonomy. To be a healthy individual, then, is to successfully navigate the waters of freedom and independence on the one hand and cooperation and selflessness on the other.

These particular theorists recognized the significant break they had made with Freud in conceiving that the bonding process has a unique constitutional base which cannot be relegated to or dismissed as sexual or strictly biological in nature. Rather, humans are, from the beginning, social, i.e., interpersonal in nature. For their health and wholeness (individuation), they must recognize their interdependence and interconnections. Psychically, as well as socially, we exist in interpersonal fields.

Still, this does not negate the reality of the self. Rather, it enriches our understanding of it. In order to balance this emphasis on the interpersonal, we next turned to self psychologists, like Guntrip and Kohut, who have drawn attention to the complexity of the self as a construct. This construct emerges early on in life, and is both discovered and created as the individual "emerges" from cycles of attachment, separation and loss. This establishes the need for an overall theoretical construct which can take account of the fundamental rhythms, the reality of positions, as Klein would call them, between first mother and child and, soon after, with others who become care-takers of various kinds.

Thus, we began with a proposal that our relational life, as a proper object of psychological study, can best be seen as developing in successive cycles of attachment, separation and loss. Each time the individual emerges from the pain of losing a former relationship with an important care-giver—that is, experiences the reality of a kind of psychic death—the individual is able to reattach to a significant other in a more healthy, mature way. Relationships which continue throughout life or for long periods progress through such cycles, if they remain healthy. In this, a self becomes more full, complete and rich. This theory of maturation and health has important consequences for how we conceive of human development, for health and psychosis, for healing and thus for ministry to persons.

The attachment cycle then makes sense from the point of view of psychoanalytic object relations theory, and from studies in the maturation process of children. Early on, in the first chapter, we proposed that it also makes sense theologically, that is, when examining a theology of ministry and healing. The importance of relating to an other, of becoming a care-taker, was highlighted. In a donation of self, the healer, minister and therapist—sometimes all three roles are incorporated by one person—experience the attachment bonding cycle. And so does the person being ministered to.

By a willingness to risk the pain of rejection and loss, in misunderstanding, poor judgment, suspicions and prejudices of all kinds which come from inevitable past injuries to the self, both the healer and the person needing healing join themselves with a God who took the same risks, suffering the same loss in the death of his Son. On the cross the God-man Jesus experienced the anxiety of annihilation, despair, and failure. His attachment to the Father, stressed in the Gospel of John, is sundered, the ultimate test of his faith and hope. And by his wounds, his followers are healed, for in his victory over death's domination a new life is born; a new kind of "being related" becomes possible. The attachment, separation, loss and rebirth cycle is vividly portrayed in the Christian Scriptures. In the Gospel story, Divinity willingly enters the human story, redeeming it of meaninglessness and saving it from despair and hopelessness. This is, for the believer, definitive proof of God's attachment to his creation.

The Christian therapist, then, understands the healing process in therapy as an entering into this mystery. It can be explained on the psychological level by the theories and studies of psychologists such as those in the object relations school within psychoanalysis. On the spiritual level it can be understood in a theology of ministry and healing which takes the dialogic and bonding process seriously. We characterized this process as first a sharing of the story and then an inclusion in the story of the other, on a more profound level.

This focus on attachment and bonding was a way of conceptualizing the propensity of human beings, as Bowlby has put it, "to make strong affectional bonds to particular others and of explaining the many forms of emotional distress and personality disturbance, including anxiety, anger, depression, and emotional detachment, to which unwilling separation and loss give rise."[2] As discussed in Chapter Two, this focus brings together the contributions of ethology and psychoanalytic theory and therapy. By combining these insights with those of object relations theorists the important rhythms and movements in relationship are given an important emphasis.

Implicit in the theology of ministry and healing sketched in Chapter One is a belief that the essence of effective nurturance and creative advancing of the "kingdom" is the daily building of relationships which are health-giving and healing, especially needed when past bonds have been ruptured through negligence, self-centeredness, or the accumulation of hurt and pain, what Christians know as the legacy of sin. Insights from the study of attachment bonding, separation anxiety and loss and mourning help the minister appreciate the normal process inherent in relationship, depicted in the ASL-R cycle. These insights hold true for the minister's consultation office, as they do for the therapist's.

Bonds develop naturally for individuals because of the universal need to be known and to know another, to feel the security of another's presence, to somehow escape the pain of anonymity and loneliness. The story which each individual claims, writes, scripts, if you will, is the story of these significant attachments, separations and losses. The hope embedded in each script, each life, is the hope of reunion, renewal or rebirth in new relationship, new life. The Christian therapist or minister when doing the work of healing ministry carries on the Jesus story and proclaims it by his or her presence and willingness to enter the life story of one in need of healing. It is the Jesus story which gives us, *par excellence*, the courage and ability to hope that rebirth and renewal is always possible. This is because in the story of the incarnation and redemption is found the "evidence" that a victory over alienation and sin has been won. In the Jesus story lies the full promise that reunion and rebirth are guaranteed to those who believe.

Christian ministry as a genuine ministry of reconciliation is then a process implying that relationships must be healed as individuals are healed. This ties a theology of healing ministry to a psychological theory of human development summarized in attachment, separation and loss terms. The hallmarks of this object relations theory and theology of ministry can be summed up in the key words: preference, persistence and periodic intensity.

Attachments are by nature to preferred individuals. Bonds created between individuals develop from and form a history of communications, caring and attention. A theology of ministry stresses the "specialness" and preferred status of the children of God. Images of God's love and his Son's love for his people in both Testaments reflect this notion of God's preference. In fact, Jesus in the New Testament time and again demonstrates a preference for those in need, for those who need healing, for those who suffer in any way from deprivation. The Beatitudes, in his Sermon on the Mount, form a litany of the preferred, or blessed (Mt 5:1–16).

In therapy, it is the special bonding which communicates to the client his or her uniqueness that is the goal of the therapist-client relationship. When the therapist is able to communicate genuine care and understanding, then the client becomes capable of examining painful relationships and issues in self-esteem.

Relationships which are nurturing and thus healing are characterized by their endurance and persistence. The cycle of attachment, separation and loss leading to renewal in relationship implies a willingness on the part of two individuals to persist in the struggle for understanding. For the believer, the example of persistence and endurance is the example of Jesus who held to his relationship with the Father despite the experience of loss and to his disciples despite their lack of fidelity. Since greater insight, maturity, and self-acceptance are possible only in traversing such cycles of attachment and loss, persistence in relationships—especially therapeutic ones—is essential for growth, whether spiritual or psychic.

Finally, there are in the ASL-R cycle, as in all relationships, periods of intensity, periods of closeness, i.e., movements toward the other as well as movements away from the other. Emotional distance is inevitable as is spiritual distance, the human tendency to pull back, to exercise freedom in relating to others or to God. Separation is not only inevitable but useful, and the anxiety it brings is an important element for growth. Since anxiety signals a danger to relationships, it is both normal and essential. The ASL-R cycle emphasizes the positive aspects of separation anxiety in fostering growth. Periodic attempts to renew the bond, to experience the comfort of an attachment figure, are not signs of regression or weakness, but rather natural movements toward the other built into the chemistry of human relationship. A natural desire to maintain bonds as well as a healthy desire to explore, venture forth into the world, is evidence of a tension built into relationships which is both psychically and spiritually nurturing.

In Chapter Six we then saw examples of how the therapeutic process involves a sharing of self, on the part of both client and therapist, and how the storied character of experience and psychic reality manifests itself in the therapeutic process. The attachment, separation, loss cycle helped provide a focus for understanding what happens in the life story of the client and what happens in the therapeutic process itself. Like all relationships which communicate the life-giving message "you matter to me" (specialness) the therapeutic relationship becomes truly significant. By becoming a care-taker, someone who provides a safe holding environment for the child or adult client, the therapist takes on significant care-taking roles and provides important security and the necessary engagement of the client. As a result, the client's self may emerge stronger and more cohesive, more mature, in having been related to an "other" whose desire it was to be an instrument for healing and strength.

Therapy, even for children, presses clients to search for the story which is uniquely theirs. It is an exercise in interiority, in self-discovery. In this process of selecting, digesting, ordering, responding and owning one's past and present, the individual whose past attachments have been damaging and painful finds strength to forge a new identity and the ability to handle the environment. Through the telling and the accepting of the story, the client breaks the barrier between the inner and outer world. And when the therapist enters into the story of the other, the therapist is offering a self as an aid in the efforts to find coherence and meaning where fragility and pain once existed. This is, as we said, always a risk for both client and therapist since it involves the real possibility of rejection and misunderstanding. But it is a risk which characterizes all growth in relationship.

The human need to belong to someone or to some group corresponds to the need to become involved in and create of oneself a meaningful story. For the Christian, it is to become involved in the most human of stories, that of the Christ, whose story is told and retold by the community of believers in an effort to remind one another of the universality of its message and the inclusiveness of its truth. The individual and the community of believers are caught up in the story of Jesus as his followers, and in living out their call to bring healing and comfort to one another they strengthen the attachment bond between one another as well as the bond between God and his creation.

▪ NOTES ▪

Introduction ▪▪

[1]J. Mack and S. Ablon, *The Development and Sustaining of Self-Esteem in Childhood* (New York: International U. Press, 1983).

[2]E. and J. Whitehead, *Method of Ministry* (New York: Seabury Press, 1983) pg. 1.

[3]S. Banks and M. Kahn, *The Sibling Bond* (New York: Basic Books, 1982) pg. 30f. *See also* J.R. Greenberg and S.A. Mitchell, *Object Relations in Psychoanalytic Theory* (Cambridge, Mass.: Harvard University Press, 1983).

[4]M. Klaus and J. Kennel, *Maternal Infant Bonding* (St. Louis: C.V. Mosby, 1977) pgs. 1–2.

[5]L. Matas, R. Arend and L. Stroufe, *Personality and Behavior Disorders* (New York: John Witney, 1984) pg. 554.

[6]H.B. Lewis, "Freud and Modern Psychiatry," *Psychoanalytic Review* 71,1, Spring 1984, pgs. 7–26, pg. 11.

[7]Lewis, op. cit., pg. 14.

[8]Lewis, op. cit., pgs. 24–27.

[9]J. Navone, *The Jesus Story: Our Life Story of Christ* (Collegeville, Minn.: Liturgical Press, 1979).

Chapter 1: Ministry and Discipleship ▪▪

[1]T. O'Meara, *A Theology of Ministry* (New York: Paulist Press, 1983) pg. 26.

[2]O'Meara, op. cit., pg. 32.

[3]K. Rahner, *A Theology of Pastoral Action* (New York: Herder and Herder, 1979).

[4]D.M. Stanley, *Jesus in Gethsemane* (New York: Paulist Press, 1979).

[5]D. Miller and D. Hadidian, *Jesus and Man's Hope* (Pittsburgh: Pittsburgh Theological Seminary, 1971), pgs. 106–117.

[6]E and J. Whitehead, *Method in Ministry,* pg. 40.

[7]K. Rahner, op. cit., pgs. 87–90.

[8]E. Schillebeeckx, *Ministry: Leadership in the Community of Jesus Christ* (New York: Crossroad, 1981) pg. 6.

[9]O'Meara, op. cit., pg. 52.

[10]O'Meara, op. cit., pg. 24.

[11]B. Cook, *Ministry to Word and Sacrament: History and Theology* (Philadelphia: Fortress Press, 1977).

[12]D. Tracy (ed.), *Toward Vatican III* (New York: Seabury, 1978) pg. 184.

[13]O'Meara, op. cit., pg. 52.

[14]Chapters 1, 2 and 11 of 1 Corinthians.

[15]M. Kelsey, *Healing and Christianity* (New York: Harper and Row, 1973).

[16]F. McNutt, *Healing* (Notre Dame, Ind.: Ave Maria Press, 1974) pg. 178.

[17]M. Linn and D. Linn, *Healing Life's Hurts* (New York: Paulist Press, 1978).

[18]M. Schurlemann, *Healing and Redemption* (St. Louis: Concordia Pub., 1965).

[19]M. Scanlan, *Inner Healing* (New York: Paulist Press, 1974).

[20]P. Tournier, *The Healing of Persons* (New York: Harper and Row, 1965).

[21]E. Bruder, *Ministry to Deeply Troubled People* (New Jersey: Prentice-Hall, 1963) pg. 29.

[22]S. Kierkegaard, *Concept of Dread* (New Jersey: Princeton University Press, 1946).

[23]Kiekegaard, op. cit., pg. 109.

[24]Don Browning, *The Moral Context of Pastoral Care* (Philadelphia, PA: Westminister Press, 1976).

[25]As long as this duty is seen in its most general aspects, then we avoid the issue of "official" versus unofficial legitimate ministries which has been in recent times the subject of much discussion.

[26]A. MacIntire, *After Virtue* (Notre Dame, Indiana: Notre Dame, 1981).

²⁷J. Navone, *Gospel Love: A Narrative Theology* (Wilmington Del.: Michael Glazier, 1984).

²⁸J. Navone, *The Jesus Story: Our Life as Story in Christ* (Collegeville, Minn.: The Liturgical Press, 1979) pg. 3.

²⁹Navone, op. cit., pg. 130.

³⁰Navone, *Gospel Love*, pg. 17.

Chapter 2: The ASL-R Cycle ▪▪

¹T. Kuhn, *The Structure of Scientific Revolutions* (Chicago: University of Chicago Press, 1962).

²J. Bowlby, *Attachment and Loss*, 3 vols. (New York: Basic Books, 1969) pgs. 73 and 80.

³Bowlby, Vol. 3 *Loss*, pg. 38.

⁴H. Harlow and M. Harlow, "Social Deprivation in Monkeys," *Scientific American* 1962 (No. 5) 207, pgs. 136–146.

⁵G.M. Eagle, *Recent Developments in Psychoanalysis* (New York: McGraw-Hill, 1984) pg. 127.

⁶J. Bowlby, *Separation*, Vol. 2, 1973.

⁷J. Bowlby, *Separation Anxiety*, Vol. 2, Attachment and Loss, 1973.

⁸S. Freud, V. 3 *Standard Edition the Complete Works of S. Freud*, Vol. 1–24, London: Hogarth, 1953–1974. All references to Freud are given in terms of his collected works in S.E.

⁹S. Freud, SE 20, pgs. 136–137.

¹⁰S. Freud, SE 1, pgs. 297ff.

¹¹S. Freud, SE 3, 1879, pg. 60.

¹²S. Freud, SE 1, pg. 297.

¹³See "Instincts and Their Vicissitudes," 1915, for his distinction among impetus, aim, object, and source of drives.

¹⁴S. Freud, SE, 4, pg. 255.

¹⁵S. Freud, SE, 7.

¹⁶S. Freud, SE, 7.

¹⁷S. Freud, SE 7, pgs. 222–223.

¹⁸S. Freud, SE 14, pg. 87.

¹⁹S. Freud, SE 18, pgs. 14–16.

²⁰S. Freud, SE 20, pgs. 137–138.

²¹S. Freud, 1940, SE 23, pg. 188.

[22]Bowlby, *Loss*, Vol 3, 1980, and J. Greenberg and S. Mitchell, *Object Relations in Psychoanalytic Theory* (Cambridge, Mass.: Harvard University Press, 1982). Also E. Jacobson, *The Self and the Object* World (New York: International University Press, 1964).

[23]Anna Freud, "Psychoanalysis and Education," *Psychoanalytic Study of the Child*, 1954, 9, pgs. 9–15.

[24]A. Freud, op. cit., pg. 47.

[25]D. Burlingham and A. Freud, *Young Children in Water* (London: Allen and Univarn, 1942), pg. 43.

[26]Burlingham and Freud, op. cit., pg. 22.

[27]M. Klein, *et al.*, *Development in Psychoanalysis* (London: Hogarth, 1952), pg. 238.

[28]Klein, op. cit., pg. 209.

[29]Klein, op. cit., pg. 243.

[30]See *Interpretation of Dreams*, Vol. 4 and 5 of SE, pgs. 605.

[31]G. Eagle, *Recent Development in Psychoanalysis*, pg. 16f.

[32]S. Freud, *Instincts and Their Vicissitudes*, SE 14, 1915, pg. 122.

[33]Eagle, op. cit., pg. 8.

[34]R. Spitz, *The First Year of Life* (New York: International University Press, 1965), pg. 90.

[35]H. Harlow, "The Nature of Love," *American Psychologist*, 13, pgs. 673–685.

[36]See D. Stern, and S. Kaplàn (eds.) writing in *Reflection of Self-Psychology* (New York: International University Press, 1984).

[37]G.F. Powell, *et al.*, "Emotional Deprivation and Growth Retardation Simulating Idiopathic Hypopitarism," *New England J. of Medicine* (1976), pgs. 276, 271–78. *See also* H. Silver and M. Finkelstein, "Deprivation Dwarfism," *J. of Pediatrics* (1970), pgs. 317–324.

[38]S. Friedman, L. Bruno and T. Vietz, "Newborn Habituation to Visual Stimuli," *J. of Experimental Child Psychology* 18 (1974), pgs. 242–51.

[39]D. Burlington and A. Freud, *Young Children in Wartime* (London: Allen and Univarn, 1942). *See also* R.A. Spitz, "Grief: A Peril in Infancy," NYU Film Library; J. Robertson and J. Robert-

son, "Young Children in Brief Separation: A First Look," *Psychoanalytic Study of the Child*, 26, pgs. 264–315.

[40]J. Bowlby, *Loss*, pg. 15.

[41]E. Kübler-Ross' work on death and dying and particularly her work with children's stages of grieving is supportive here.

[42]S. Freud, SE 13, pg. 65.

[43]Bowlby, *Loss*, op. cit., pg. 27.

[44]S. Freud, SE 14, pgs. 250, 256.

[45]Bowlby, *Loss*, op. cit., pg. 247.

[46]G. Eagle, "Is Grief a Disease?" *Psychoanalytic Med:23*, pgs. 18–22.

Chapter 3: Human Relationship in the Developmental Process ■■

[1]H.S. Sullivan, *The Fusion of Psychiatry and the Social Sciences* (New York: Norton, 1964) pg. 302.

[2]J. Greenberg, S. Mitchell, *Object Relations in Psychoanalytic Theory* (Cambridge, Mass.: Harvard University Press, 1983), pg. 79.

[3]H.S. Sullivan, *Interpersonal Theory of Psychiatry* (New York: Norton, 1924 and 1953).

[4]H.S. Sullivan, *Schizophrenia as a Human Process* (New York: Norton, 1925 and 1962), pg. 92–93.

[5]In this his approach differs from the object relations school of thought. Those theorists taken up in the next chapter have stressed that internal objects and processes with a presumed personal referent can be studied in language and vocabulary. Language and vocabulary, because of his experience with psychotics, could easily mislead, he felt.

[6]H.S. Sullivan, *Conceptions of Modern Psychiatry* (New York: Norton, 1940), pg. 10.

[7]H.S. Sullivan, *Interpersonal Theory of Psychiatry*, pg. 34.

[8]Greenberg, Mitchell, op. cit., pg. 96.

[9]H.S. Sullivan, *The Fusion of Psychiatry and the Social Sciences*, pg. 36.

[10]M. Klein, *Fusion of Psychiatry and Social Sciences*, pg. 219.

[11]H. Guntrip, *Psychoanalytic Theory, Therapy and the Self* (New York: Basic Books, 1971), pgs. 3–15.

[12]Guntrip, op. cit., pg. 60.

[13]Guntrip and Fairbairn feel that the paranoid-schizoid position is actually two separate positions. In the schizoid, the infant is actually withdrawn from the object, whereas in the paranoid, while in relationship, the infant feels persecuted.

[14]M. Klein, *Contributions to Psychoanalysis* (New York: McGraw-Hill, 1964).

[15]M. Klein, *Envy and Gratitude and Other Works* (New York: Delacorte Press, 1948 and 1975), pg. 34.

[16]M. Klein, *Contributions to Psychoanalysis*, pg. 290.

[17]M. Klein, op. cit., pg. 310.

[18]The presupposition of extensive constitutional knowledge and imagery present shortly after birth is unconvincing to many. For example, see Fairbairn, 1952, pg. 154; Mitchell and Greenberg, 1983, pg. 148; Modell, 1968, pg. 120.

[19]D. Jackson, "The Question of Family Homeostasis," *Psychiatric Quarterly*, Suppl. 31: 1957, pgs. 79–90.

[20]G. Bateson, *Mind and Nature: A Necessary Unit* (New York: Dutton, 1979).

"A Note on the Double Bind," *Family Process*, 2: 1962, pgs. 154–161.

[21]S. Slipp, *Object Relations: A Dynamic Bridge Between Individual and Family Treatment* (New York: Jason Aronson, 1984), pg. 3.

[22]R. Lange, *The Bipersonal Field* (New York: Jason Aronson, 1976).

[23]S. Ferenczi, *Further Contributions to the Theory and Technique of Psychoanalysis* (London: Hogarth Press, 1920). See especially his chapter, "Further Development of an Active Therapy in Psychoanalysis."

[24]Ferenczi analyzed Klein and so had a profound impact on the direction of her work and her theory.

[25]S. Slipp, *Object Relations*, pgs. 41–45.

[26]It is important to distinguish projective identification from pure projection. In pure projection, firm ego boundaries may exist. For the other is seen and experienced only in terms of inner

feelings and images that are transferred. The projector does not feel "connected" to the object, in other words. Rather, the object is separate, even threatening. In addition, no effort is made to induce, influence or control the other in pure projection.

[27]See, for example, S. Minuchin, *Family Systems Therapy: An Integration* (New York: Jason Aronson, 1984), which stresses analysis of the system in its present functioning state.

[28]See B. Montalvo and J. Haley's paradoxically titled article, "In Defense of Child Therapy," *Family Process*, 12, #3, Sept. 1973, pgs. 227–244, in which they contend that work in the individual child is really a family systems approach.

Chapter 4: The Developmental Cycle in Object Relations Theory ▪▪

[1]I.D. Suttie, *The Origins of Love and Hate* (London: Kegan Paul, 1935).

[2]M. Mahler, *On Human Symbiosis and the Vicissitudes of Individuation*, Vol. 1 (New York: International University Press, 1968), pg. 42.

[3]Mahler, op. cit., pg. 9.

[4]M. Mahler, *et al.*, *The Psychological Birth of the Human Infant* (New York: Basic Books, 1975), pg. 55.

[5]E. Jacobson, *The Self and the Object World* (New York: International University Press, 1964).

[6]R. Spitz, *The First Year of Life: A Psychological Study of Normal and Deviant Development of Object Relations* (New York: International University Press, 1965).

[7]Mahler, op. cit., pg. 47.

[8]M. Mahler, "On Symbiotic Child Psychoses," *Psychoanalytic Study of the Child, Vol.* 10 (New York: International University Press, 1955), pgs. 195–212.

[9]Mahler, *et al.*, pg. 206.

[10]Mahler, *et al.*, pg. 118.

[11]Slipp, op. cit., p. 51. See also O. Kernberg, *Internal and External World* (New York: Jason Aronson, 1980). The term "self object" is taken from Kohut, who uses it to refer to undifferentiated family relations.

[12]M. Mahler, *et al.* op. cit, p. 108.

[13]D.W. Winnicott, *Playing and Reality* (Middlesex, England: Penguin, 1971), pg. 115.

[14]D.W. Winnicott, *Through Pediatrics to Psychoanalysis* (London: Hogarth, 1958), pg. 304.

[15]D.W. Winnicott, *Maturation Process and the Facilitating Environment* (New York: International University Press, 1965), pg. 34.

[16]C. Gilligan, *In a Different Voice* (Cambridge, Mass.: Harvard University Press, 1981).

[17]D.W. Winnicott, *Through Pediatrics to Psychoanalysis*, pg. 304.

[18]D.W. Winnicott, op. cit., pg. 246.

[19]D.W. Winnicott, *Maturation Process and the Facilitating Environment*, pg. 34.

[20]D.W. Winnicott, op. cit., pg. 147.

[21]D.W. Winnicott, *The Family and Individual Development* (London: Hogarth Tavistock, 1965), pg. 46.

[22]This is a principal feature of the first creation myth recorded in Genesis, where the command to "increase and multiply, to have dominion," etc., is given to creation from the Creator as part of what it means to be creation.

[23]D.W. Winnicott, *Maturation Process and the Facilitating Environment*, pg. 182.

[24]*Psychoanalytic Study of Personality* (London: Tavistock, 1952), pg. 137.

[25]Eagle, *New Developments in Psychoanalysis*, pg. 79.

[26]Introjection, in Freud's terminology, differs somewhat from the way Fairbairn uses it. Fairbairn discusses introjection in relation to superego prohibition, punishments and evaluations once experienced in relation to an external object. These are introjected and made part of the self and to a degree are experienced as such. Even still, these are experienced as foreign at times.

[27]W.R.D. Fairbairn, *Object Relations Theory of Personality* (New York: Basic Books, 1952).

[28]Greenberg and Mitchell, *Object Relations in Psychoanalytic Theory*, pg. 154.

[29]Fairbairn, op. cit., pg. 149f.

[30]Fairbairn, op. cit., pg. 33.

[31]Fairbairn, op. cit., pg. 34.

[32]Fairbairn, op. cit., pg. 48.

[33]Fairbairn, op. cit., pg. 148.

[34]Greenberg and Mitchell, op. cit., pg. 163.

[35]O. Kernberg, *Borderline Condition and Pathological Narcissisms* (New York: Jason Aronson, 1975).

Chapter 5: The Development of Self-Esteem ▪▪

[1]J. Kagan, "Emergence of Self," *Annual Progress in Child Psychiatry and Child Development*, S. Chess and A. Thomas, eds. (New York: Brunner/Mazel, 1983), pg. 5–28.

[2]J. Kagan, op. cit., pg. 26.

[3]J. Mack and S. Ablon, eds. *The Development and Sustaining of Self-Esteem in Childhood* (New York: International University Press, 1983).

[4]See G. Bateson, "The Cybernetics of Self: A Theory of Alcoholism," in *Steps to an Ecology of the Mind* (New York: Valentine Books, 1971), pgs. 307–37, and pg. 319.

[5]Cited in P. Elson, "Parenthood and the Transformations of Narcissism," *Parenthood: A Psychoanalytic Perspective*, R. Cohen, B. Cohler and S. Weissman, eds. (New York: The Guilford Press, 1984), pg. 299.

[6]J. Huizenga, "The Relationship of Self-Esteem and Narcissism," *The Development and Sustaining of Self-Esteem in Childhood*, eds. J. Mack and S. Ablon (New York: International University Press, 1983), pg. 151.

[7]H. Kohut and E.S. Wolf, "The Disorders of the Self and Their Treatment: An Outline," *International Journal of Psychoanalysis*, 59 (413) 413–425, 1978.

[8]"Parenthood and the Transformation of Narcissism," in *Parenthood: A Psychodynamic Perspective*, R. Cohen, B. Choler, S. Weismann, eds., 1984.

[9]H. Kohut, *The Analysis of the Self* (New York: International University Press, 1971).

[10]Mack and Ablon (eds.), 1983.

[11]H.S. Sullivan, *Interpersonal Theory of Psychiatry*, Vol. 1, Collected Works (New York: Norton), pg. 165.

[12]N. Cotton, *"The Development of Self-Esteem and Self-Esteem Regulation,"* Mack and Ablon, eds., op. cit. pg. 123.

[13]N. Cotton, op. cit., pg. 124.

[14]S. Coopersmith, *The Antecedents of Self-Esteem* (San Francisco: Freeman, 1967).

[15]Mahler, Pine and Bergman, *The Psychological Birth of the Human Infant: Symbiosis and Introduction*, 1975, pg. 269.

[16]N. Cotton, op. cit., pg. 131.

[17]M. Rosenberg, *Conceiving the Self* (New York: Basic Books, 1979).

[18]M. Rosenberg, op. cit., pg. 74.

[19]See A. Miller, *Prisoners of Childhood* (New York: Basic Books, 1981), and H. Kohut, *The Analysis of the Self* (New York: International University Press, 1971).

[20]N. Chodorow, *The Reproduction of Mothering: Psychoanalysis and the Sociology of Gender* (Berkeley, Cal.: University of California Press, 1978).

[21]Deutch, *The Psychology of Woman* (1925) (New York: Bantam, 1973), pg. 165.

[22]Deutch, op. cit., pg. 193.

[23]C. Gilligan, *In a Different Voice* (1982).

[24]M. Buber, *I and Thou*, 2nd revised edition (New York: Charles Scribner's Sons, 1958).

[25]See also F. Givlerber, "The Parent-Child Relationship and the Development of Self-Esteem," in Mack and Ablon (eds.), op. cit.

[26]M. Kahn and S. Banks, *The Sibling Bond* (New York: Basic Books, 1982).

[27]Ibid., pp. 30–31.

[28]See G. Eagle's discussion in *Recent Developments in Psychoanalysis.* He especially cites the work of Milton Klein, "On Mahler's Autistic and Symbiotic Phases: An Exposition and Evaluation." *In Psychoanalysis and Contemporary Thought*, 1981, 4, 69–105.

[29]See Peter Stratton's discussion in "Biological Preprogramming of Infant Behavior" and Susan Goldberg's "Parent-Infant Bonding: Another Look," both in *Annual Progress In Child Psychiatry and Child Development*, S. Chess and A. Thomas, eds. (New York: Brunner/Mazel, 1985).

[30]V. Frankl, *Man's Search For Meaning* (New York: Simon and Schuster, 1970).

[31]H. Clinebell, *Basic Types of Pastoral Counseling* (Nashville, Tenn.: Abingdon, 1966, 1984), pg. 25f.

[32]Ibid., pg. 31.

[33]See C. Rogers, *Client Centered Therapy* (Boston: Houghton Mifflin, 1951).

Chapter 6: The Attachment Cycle and Therapy ▪▪

[1]P. Collins and R. Hayes, "Education of the Imagination," *J. of Humanistic Education and Development*, 22, 2–7.

[2]S. Gladding, "Counseling and Creative Arts," *Counseling and Human Development*, Vol. 18, 1, Sept. 1985.

[3]J. DiLeo, *Children's Drawings as Diagnostic Aids* (New York: Brunner/Mazel, 1973). *Interpreting Children's Drawings*, (New York: Brunner/Mazel, 1983). F.L. Goodenough, *Measurement of Intelligence by Drawings* (New York: World Book Co., 1926). R. Kellogg, *Analyzing Children's Art* (Palo Alto, Cal.: National Press Book, 1970). H. B. Landgasten, *Clinical Art Therapy: A Comprehensive Guide* (New York: Brunner/Mazel, 1981).

[4]DiLeo, *Children's Drawings as Diagnostic Aids*.

[5]H. Kivnick, J. Erickson, "The Arts as Healing," *American J. of Orthopsychiatry*, 53, 4, Oct. 1983, 602–618.

[6]Op. cit., p. 617.

[7]R. Driekurs, "Family Group Therapy within The Chicago Guidance Center," *Mental Hygiene*, 35, 1951, pgs. 291–301.

[8]E. Weinrib, *Images of Self* (Boston, Mass.: Sigo Press, 1983). F. Wiches, *The Inner World of the Childhood* (New Jersey: Prentice-Hall, 1966).

[9]N. Ackerman, *Treating the Troubled Family* (New York: Basic Books, 1966).

[10]M. Friedman, *The Healing Dialogue in Psychotherapy* (New York: Jason Aronson, 1985), pg. xl.

[11]M. Buber, *The Knowledge of Man: A Philosophy of the Interhuman* (New York: Harper and Row, 1966), pg. 181f.

[12]R. Greenson, *The Technique and Practice of Psychoanalysis* (New York: International University Press, 1967), pp. 151–152.

[13]H. Kohut, *Analysis of the Self,* op. cit.

[14]O. Kernberg, "Notes on the Countertransference," *Journal of American Psychoanalytic Association,* 13, 38–56.

[15]C. Rogers, *Client-Centered Therapy* (Boston: Houghton-Mifflin, 1951).

Chapter 7: Overall Summary ▪▪

[1]See Lecture 32, "Anxiety and the Instinctual Life." In *New Introductory Lectures on Psychoanalysis,* op. cit.

[2]J. Bowlby, "The Making and Breaking of Affectional Bonds" *British J. of Psychiatry,* 1977, 130, 200–210, and 421–431.

■ BIBLIOGRAPHY ■

Ackerman, N. (1966) *Treating the Troubled Family.* N.Y.: Basic Books.

Bateson, G. (1979) *Mind and Nature: A Necessary Unit.* N.Y.: Dutton.

―――― (1962) "A Note on the Double Bind." *Family Process.* 2: 154–161.

―――― (1971) "The Cybernetics of Self: A Theory of Alcoholism." *Steps to an Ecology of the Mind.* N.Y.: Valentine Books.

Bowlby, J. (1969) *Attachment and Loss,* vol. 3. N.Y.: Basic Books.

―――― (1973) vol. 2, *Separation: Anxiety and Anger.* N.Y.: Basic Books.

―――― (1980) vol. 3, *Loss: Sadness and Depression.* N.Y.: Basic Books.

―――― (1977) "The Making and Breaking of Affectional Bonds." *British J. of Psychiatry.* 130, 200–210, and 421–431.

Browning, D. *The Moral Context of Pastoral Care.* (1976) Philadelphia, PA: Westminister.

Buber, M. (1966) *The Knowledge of Man: A Philosophy of the Interhuman.* N.Y.: Harper and Row.

Bruder, E. (1963) *Ministry to Deeply Troubled People.* N.Y.: Prentice-Hall.

Burlingham, D. and Freud, A. (1942) *Young Children in Wartime.* London: Allen and Unwyn.

Chodorow, N. (1978) *The Reproduction of Mothering: Psychoanalysis and the Sociology of Gender.* Berkeley, CA: University of California.

Collins, P. and Hayes, R. "Education of the Imagination." *J. of Humanistic Education and Development.* 22, 2–7.

Cook, B. (1977) *Ministry to Word and Sacrament.* Philadelphia, PA: Fortress Press.

179

Coopersmith, S. (1967) *The Antecedents of Self-Esteem.* San Francisco, CA: Freeman.

Cotten, N. (1983) "The Development of Self-Esteem and Self-Esteem Regulation." *The Development and Sustaining of Self-Esteem.* Mack, J. and Ablon, S. (eds.) N.Y.: International U. Press.

Deutch, H. (1925) *The Psychology of Women: A Psychoanalytic Interpretation.* N.Y.: Bantam Books.

DiLeo, J. (1973) *Children's Drawings as Diagnostic Aids.* N.Y.: Brunner/Mazel.

———— (1983) *Interpreting Children's Drawings.* N.Y.: Brunner/Mazel.

Dreikurs, R. (1951) "Family Group Therapy Within the Chicago Guidance Center." *Mental Hygiene.* 35: 291–301.

Eagle, G. (1984) *Recent Developments in Psychoanalysis.* N.Y.: McGraw-Hill.

———— "Is Grief a Disease?" *Psychoanalytic Medicine.* 23: 18–22.

Elson, P. (1984) "Parenthood and the Transformations of Narcissism." *Parenthood: Psychoanalytic Perspective.* Cohen, *et al.* (eds). N.Y.: Guiford Press.

Fairbairn, W.R.D. (1952) *Object Relations Theory of Personality.* N.Y.: Basic Books.

Ferenczi, S. (1952) *The Psychoanalytic Study of Personality.* London: Hogarth-Tavistock.

———— (1920) *Further Contributions to the Theory and Technique of Psychoanalysis.* London: Hogarth-Tavistock.

Friedman, M. (1985) *The Healing Dialogue in Psychotherapy.* N.Y.: Jason Aronson.

Friedman, S., *et al.* (1974) "The Newborn Habituation to Visual Stimuli." *J. of Experimental Child Psychology.* 18: 242–251.

Freud, A. (1954) "Psychoanalysis and Education." *Psychoanalytic Study of the Child.* 9: 9–15.

Freud, A. and Burlingham, D. (1944) *Infants Without Families.* N.Y.: International U. Press.

Freud, S. *Standard Edition of the Collected Works of Sigmund Freud.* vols. 1–24. London: Hogarth Press. 1953–1974. (S.E.)

———— (1894) *The Neuro-Psychoses of Defense.* S.E. 3

———— (1895) *Project for a Scientific Psychology,* S.E. 1

———— (1900) *The Interpretation of Dreams.* S.E. 4 and 5

———— (1905) *Three Essays on a Theory of Sexuality.* S.E. 7

———— (1910) *A Special Type of Choice Object.* S.E. 11

———— (1912–13) *Totem and Taboo.* S.E. 13

———— (1914) *On Narcissism.* S.E. 14

———— (1915) *Instincts and Their Vicissitudes.* S.E. 14

———— (1917) *Mourning and Melancholia.* S.E. 14

———— (1920) *Beyond the Pleasure Principle.* S.E. 18

———— (1921) *Group Psychology and the Analysis of the Ego.* S.E. 18

———— (1923) *The Ego and the Id.* S.E. 19

———— (1926) *Inhibitions, Symptoms and Anxiety.* S.E. 20

———— (1930) *Civilization and Its Discontents.* S.E. 21

———— (1933) *New Introductory Lectures on Psycho-Analysis.* S.E. 22

———— (1937–39) *Moses and Monotheism.* S.E. 23

Gilligan, C. (1981) *In a Different Voice.* Cambridge, MA: Harvard U. Press.

Gladding, S. (1985) "Counseling and Creative Arts." *Counseling and Human Development.* vol. 18, 1.

Goodenough, F.L. (1926) *Measurement of Intelligence by Drawings.* N.Y.: World Book Co.

Greenberg, J. and Mithell, S. (1983) *Object Relations in Psychoanalytic Theory.* Cambridge, MA: Harvard U. Press.

Greenson, R. (1967) *The Technique and Practice of Psychoanalysis.* N.Y.: International U. Press.

Guntrip, H. (1971) *Psychoanalytic Theory, Therapy and the Self.* N.Y.: Basic Books.

Harlow, H. "The Nature of Love." *American Psychologist.* 13: 673–685.

Harlow, H. and Harlow, M. (1962) "Social Deprivation in Monkeys." *Scientific American.* 5: 136–146.

Huizenga, J. (1983) "The Relationship of Self-Esteem and Narcissism." *The Development and Sustaining of Self-Esteem in Childhood.* Mack, J. and Ablon, S. (eds.) N.Y.: International U. Press.

Jackson, D. (1957) "The Question of Family Homeostasis." *Psychiatric Quarterly.* suppl. 31: 79–90.

Jacobson, E. (1964) *The Self and the Object World.* N.Y.: International U. Press.

Kagan, J. (1983) "The Emergence of the Self." *Annual Progress in Child Psychiatry and Child Development.* Chess, S. and Thomas, A. (eds.) N.Y.: Brunner/Mazel.

Kellogg, R. (1970) *Analyzing Children's Art.* Palo Alto, CA: National Press Books.

Kelsey, M. (1973) *Healing and Christianity.* N.Y.: Harper and Row.

Kernberg, O. "Notes on Countertransference." *J. of American Psychoanalytic Assoc.* 13:38–56.

———— (1980) *Internal World and External Reality.* N.Y.: Jason Aronson.

———— (1975) *The Borderline Condition and Pathological Narcissism.* N.Y.: Jason Aronson.

Kierkegaard, S. (1946) *The Concept of Dread.* N.J.: Princeton U. Press.

Klaus, M. and Kennel, J. (1977) *Mother-Infant Bonding.* St. Louis: C.V. Mosby.

Klein, M. (1964) *Contributions to Psychoanalysis.* N.Y.: McGraw-Hill.

———— (1948) *Envy and Gratitude and Other Works.* N.Y. Delacorte Press.

———— (1952) *Developments in Psychoanalysis.* London: Hogarth.

Kivnick, H., H. and Erikson, J. (1984) "The Arts as Healing." *American J. of Orthopsychiatry.* 53(4): 602–617.

Kohut, H. (1971) *The Analysis of the Self.* N.Y.: International U. Press.

Kohut, H. and Wolf, S. (1978) "The Disorders of the Self and Their Treatment: An Outline." *International J. of Psychoanalysis.* 59:413–425.

Kübler-Ross, E. (1983) *On Children and Death.* N.Y.: Macmillan.

Kuhn, T. (1962) *The Structure of Scientific Revolutions.* Chicago: U. of Chicago Press.

Landgarten, H.B. (1981) *Clinical Art Therapy: A Comprehensive Guide.* N.Y.: Brunner/Mazel.

Lange, R. (1976) *The Bipersonal Field.* N.Y.: Jason Aronson.

Lewis, H.B. (1984) "Freud and Modern Psychiatry." *Psychoanalytic Review.* 71,L: 7–26.

Linn, M. and Linn, D. (1978) *Healing Life's Hurts.* N.Y.: Paulist Press.

Mack, J. and Ablon, S. (1983) *The Development and Sustaining of Self-Esteem in Childhood.* N.Y.: International U. Press.

Mahler, M. (1968) *On Symbiosis and the Vicissitudes of Individuation.* N.Y.: International U. Press.

Mahler, M., *et al.* (1975) *The Psychological Birth of the Human Infant.* N.Y.: International U. Press.

MacIntire, A. (1981) *After Virtue.* Notre Dame, IN: Notre Dame Press.

Matas, L., *et al.* (1984) *Personality and Behavior Disorders.* N.Y.: John Whitney.

McNutt, F. (1974) *Healing.* Notre Dame, IN: Ave Maria Press.

Miller, A. (1981) *Prisoners of Childhood.* N.Y.: Basic Books.

Miller, D. and Hadidian, D. (1971) *Jesus and Man's Hope.* Pittsburgh, PA: Pittsburgh Theological Seminary.

Minuchin, S. (1968) *Family Systems Therapy: An Integration.* N.Y.: Jason Aronson.

Modell, A. *Object Love and Reality.* N.Y.: International U. Press.

Montalvo, B. and Haley, J. (1973) "In Defense of Child Therapy." *Family Process.* 12, no. 3: 227–244.

Navone, J. (1979) *The Jesus Story: Our Life and Story in Christ.* Collegeville, MN: The Liturgical Press.

———(1984) *Gospel Love: A Narrative Theology.* Wilmington, DE: Michael Glazier.

O'Meara, T. (1983) *A Theology of Ministry.* N.Y.: Paulist Press.

Powell, G. *et al.* (1976) "Emotional Deprivation and Growth Retardation." *New England J. of Medicine.* 271–78.

Rahner, K. (1979) *A Theology of Pastoral Action.* N.Y.: Herder and Herder.

Robertson, J. and Robertson, J. "Young Children in Brief Separation: A First Look." *Psychoanalytic Study of the Child.* 26:264–315.

Rogers, C. (1951) *Client-Centered Therapy.* Boston: Houghton Mifflin.

Rosenberg, M. (1979) *Conceiving the Self.* N.Y.: Basic Books.

Scanlan, M. (1974) *Inner Healing.* N.Y.: Paulist Press.

Schillebeeckx, E. (1981) *Ministry: Leadership in the Community of Jesus.* N.Y.: Crossroad.

Schurlemann, M. (1965) *Healing and Redemption.* St. Louis: Concordia Publications.

Silver, H. and Finkelstein, M. (1970) "Deprivation Dwarfism." *J. of Pediatrics.* 317–324.

Slipp, S. (1984) *Object Relations: A Dynamic Bridge Between Individual and Family Treatment.* N.Y.: Jason Aronson.

Spitz, R. Grief: "Peril in Infancy." NYU Film Library.

——— (1965) *The First Year of Life.* N.Y.: International U. Press.

Stanley, D. (1979) *Jesus in Gethsemane.* N.Y.: Paulist Press.

Sullivan, H.S. (1964) *The Fusion of Psychiatry and the Social Sciences.* N.Y.: Norton.

——— (1924, 1953) *Interpersonal Theory of Psychiatry.* N.Y.: Norton.

——— (1925, 1962) *Schizophrenia as a Human Process.* N.Y.: Norton.

——— (1940) *Conceptions of Modern Psychiatry.* N.Y.: Norton.

Suttie, I. (1935) *The Origins of Love and Hate.* London: Kegan Paul.

Tournier, P. (1965) *The Healing of Persons.* N.Y.: Harper and Row.

Tracy, D. (ed.) (1978) *Toward Vatican III.* N.Y.: Seabury.

Weinrib, E. (1983) *Images of the Self.* Boston, MA: Sigo Press.

Whitehead, E. and Whitehead, J. (1983) *Method in Ministry.* N.Y.: Seabury.

Whickes, F. (1966) *The Inner World of Childhood.* N.J.: Prentice-Hall.

Winnicott, D.W. (1971) *Playing and Reality.* Middlesex, ENG: Penguin.

——— (1965) *The Family and Individual Development.* London: Hogarth.

——— (1965) *The Maturational Process and the Facilitating Environment.* N.Y.: International U. Press.

——— (1958) *Through Pediatrics to Psychoanalysis.* London: Hogarth.

■ AUTHOR INDEX ■

Ablon, S.   102, 167, 175, 183
Ackerman, N.   135, 177, 179
Ainsworth   9, 10

Balint; developmental arrest   90; and
   Freud   159–60; "primary love object"
   49
Banks, S.   111, 167
Bateson, Gregory   69, 172, 175, 179
Bowlby, John   10, 33, 34–35, 40, 45, 50,
   51, 52, 159–60, 163, 169, 170, 171, 178,
   179
Browning, Don   24–25, 168, 179
Bruder, E.   24, 168
Buber, Martin   109, 147, 176, 177, 179
Burlingham, D.   46, 50, 170, 179

Chodorow, N.; criticisms of object
   relations view   106–109; writings of
   176, 179
Clinebell, H.   113, 177
Cohen, R.   102, 175
Collins, P.   117, 177, 179
Congar, Yves   14
Cook, Bernard   18, 168, 179
Coopersmith, S.   104, 176, 180
Cotten, N.   103, 180

Darwin, Charles; influence upon Freud
   42
Deutsch, H.   107, 176, 180
DiLeo, J.   117–18, 177, 180
Dreikurs, R.   134, 177, 180

Eagle, G.   47, 49, 94–95, 170, 171, 174,
   176, 180
Erikson, Erik   103, 119

Fairbairn, W.R.D.   49, 68, 79, 90, 100, 101,
   161, 172, 174, 175, 180; coping with
   ambiguity   92–95; developmental
   theory of   96, 97, 109–10, 112; "primary
   identification"   103; theory of
   motivation   95–96
Ferenczi, Sandor   69–70, 81, 172, 180

Finkelstein, M.   49, 170, 184
Frankl, Viktor   113, 177
Freud, Anna   45, 170, 179, 180
Freud, Sigmund; human emotional bonds
   10–11, 32, 40, 43–49, 50, 54–55, 73, 80, 81;
   modifications of his theories. See Klein,
   M. and Sullivan, H.S.; and mourning
   50–52; psychoanalytic framework   41–
   43, 44; psychodynamic theory   33–35,
   64, 104, 147; writings of   170, 171, 180–
   81
Friedman, S.   143–44, 147, 170, 180

Gilligan, Carol; and moral development
   89, 108; and self-definition   108;
   writings of 176, 180
Gladding, S.   117, 177, 180
Goodenough, F.L.   117, 177, 180
Greenberg, J.R.   45, 58, 61, 167, 171, 174,
   175, 181
Greenson, 152–53, 177, 181
Guntrip, H.   63, 64, 65, 90, 94, 161, 172,
   181
Gustafson, James M.   16

Harlow, H. and M.   10, 36, 48, 169, 170,
   181
Hayes, R.   117, 177
Huizenga, J.   101, 175, 181

Jackson, Donald; influenced by Klein and
   Sullivan   68; theories of   69; writings
   of   172, 182
Jacobson, E.   45, 80, 83, 173, 182
James, William; influence upon H.S.
   Sullivan   59, 60

Kagan, Jerome   99–100, 103, 104, 175, 182
Kellogg, R.   117, 177, 182
Kelsey, Morton   22, 168, 182
Kennell, J.   9, 167, 182
Kernberg, Otto   97–98, 156, 173, 175, 178,
   182
Kierkegaard, Søren   24, 168, 182
Klaus, M.   9, 167, 182

Klein, Melanie; background of   57; family
    relations theory   68–77; intrapsychic
    life of child   63, 66, 93; modification of
    Freud's theory   5–6, 46, 48, 51, 62–66,
    160–61; theories of   63–77, 88, 91, 96,
    109; writings of   170, 172, 182
Kivnick, H.   119
Kohut, H.   93, 101, 110–11, 156, 161, 175,
    178, 182
Kübler-Ross, Elisabeth   22, 50, 171, 182
Kuhn, Thomas   34, 111, 169, 182

Landgasten, H. B.   117, 177, 182
Lange, Robert; "bipersonal field theory"
    69; influenced by Klein and Sullivan
    68; writings of   172, 182
Lewis, Helen B.; understanding of Freud
    10–11; writings of   167, 183
Linn, D. and M.   22, 168, 183

Mack, J.   100–101, 102, 167, 175, 183
Mahler, Margaret   10, 45, 59, 68, 78, 79,
    109, 111–12, 116, 161; and Fairbairn
    93, 109; individuation   53, 80–88, 104,
    126; role of mother   78; writings of
    173, 174, 176, 183
MacIntire, Alister   26, 168, 183
McNutt, Francis   22, 168, 183

Navone, John   12, 27–28, 167, 169, 183

O'Meara, Thomas   14, 18, 19, 167, 168,
    183

Paul, Saint; and ministry   18–22, 168

Piaget, Jean   103
Powell, G.F.   49, 170, 183

Rahner, Karl; and ministry   14, 16–17;
    writings of   167, 168, 183
Rogers, Carl   158, 177, 178, 183
Rosenberg, M.   104–105, 176, 183

Scanlan, M.   23, 168, 184
Schillebeeckx, Edward; and ministry   14,
    17; writings of   168, 184
Schurlemann, M.   22–23, 184
Shea, John   18
Silver, H.   49, 170, 184
Slipp, S.; influenced by Klein and Sullivan
    68, 72; writings of   172, 173, 184
Spitz, R. A.   10, 47–48, 50, 80, 83, 171, 173,
    184
Stanley, D. M.   20, 167, 184
Stern, D.   48–49, 170
Stroufe   9, 10, 167
Sullivan, H.S.; family relations theory
    68–77, 93; infant-caretaker relationship
    60, 61–63; interpersonal theory of   57–
    63, 88, 111, 112; response to Freudian
    psychodynamic theory   5–6, 56–59, 62–
    63, 160; writings of   171, 175, 184
Suttie, I.D.   80, 173, 184

Tournier, R.   24, 168, 184

Whitehead, Evelyn and James   3, 167,
    168, 184
Winnicott, D.W.   72, 78, 79, 85, 109, 111,
    161, 174, 184; "the holding environment"
    88–92

■ SUBJECT INDEX ■

ambiguity; and Fairbairn   92–95; and
    Kernberg   98
anxiety   60–61, 163
attachment; bonds of   35, 36–38, 48;
    defined   9, 35, 47–49, 80, 98, 162;
    mother-infant bond   43–47, 59–60; *See
    also* family relations theory; related to
    healing   26, 115, 164; and therapy
    115–16

countertransference   155–57

disintegration   53, 61

ego; Fairbairn's understanding of   93–95
emotions   36–39
ethology; defined   36; evidence from
    48

family relations theory   68–77, 173

grieving   50
growth cycle   6–9, 32; *See also*
    attachment, mourning, separation,
    Chapter 2 on ASL-R Cycle

healing, ministry of; overview of   7, 12;
    and projective drawings   117ff.; rooted
    in Jesus   15–16, 19–20, 23, 26, 27, 163–
    164, 166; and Scripture   15–16, 18–26,
    114, 162–63; theology of   13–16, 22–26,
    31–32; and therapy   109–11, 113, 115–
    16, 120–58, 162–63, 165–66

individuation   53, 67, 80–88, 99, 100–101,
    133
interaction, explained   79, 88
introjection   95, 174

melancholia   52, 53
ministry, theology of   14–32, 163;
    criterion for authentic ministry   16–18;
    and healing   22–26, 114; and narrative
    theology   26–32;   Scriptural
    approaches 18–26

mother-infant bond; *See* attachment,
    Freud, Klein, Sullivan, names of
    individual theorists, family relations
    theory
motivation, Fairbairn's theory of   95–96
mourning   50–54

narrative theology (theology of story);
    explained   3, 27–32; and theology of
    ministry   26–27

"object relations"; criticisms of   106–109;
    defined and explained   4–5, 11, 43, 78–
    80, 99–100, 162; and development of
    self-esteem   102–106; and family
    relations   69, 74; and Freudian
    psychodynamic theory   11, 34, 43, 68;
    and self   100–102; and theology of
    ministry   9, 74–75; *See also* Fairbairn,
    Mahler, Winnicott

pathology   96
"primary object love"   49
projective drawings   117–20, 121ff., 138ff.
projective identification   70–74, 172–173
psychoanalytic framework, and Freud
    41–47
psychodynamic theory; explained and
    described   7–9, 32; Freudian
    paradigm   34–35, 47, 54–55; two
    schools resulting from Freud   11, 34

rapprochement   85–88, 110
reconciliation, ministry of   13, 18–22, 164

self-esteem, development of   102–106,
    109
"self-system," explained   62
separation; as part of growth cycle   7, 32,
    37–39, 49–54, 66–67, 99, 133; and
    individuation (Mahler's theory)   80–88,
    116–17; and Winnicott's theory   90–91;
    See also grieving, growth cycle,
    mourning

symbiosis, defined   81–83, 85–86,
   131–33

theological reflection; and healing   7–9,
   13–16, 22–26; and psychologists   3–4,
   11–12; and Scripture   3, 14, 15, 27–32;
   three sources for   3; Whitehead's

methodology   3
theory of motivation, anxiety, and
   defenses   40–41, 60–61, 95–96
therapy; and attachment cycle   115, 128–
   33; and healing of self   109–14, 121–35;
   and projective drawings   117ff.
transference   152–57